DATE DUE			
Dec 13'71			

THE CONQUEST OF NEW FRANCE

TEXTBOOK EDITION

∴

THE CHRONICLES
OF AMERICA SERIES
ALLEN JOHNSON
EDITOR

GERHARD R. LOMER
CHARLES W. JEFFERYS
ASSISTANT EDITORS

THE SIEGE OF LOUISBOURG, 1745

From the painting by C. W. Jefferys

THE CONQUEST
OF NEW FRANCE

A CHRONICLE OF THE
COLONIAL WARS
BY GEORGE M. WRONG

NEW HAVEN: YALE UNIVERSITY PRESS
TORONTO: GLASGOW, BROOK & CO.
LONDON: HUMPHREY MILFORD
OXFORD UNIVERSITY PRESS
1921

CONTENTS

I. THE CONFLICT OPENS: FRONTE-
NAC AND PHIPS   Page   1

II. QUEBEC AND BOSTON   "   24

III. FRANCE LOSES ACADIA   "   44

IV. LOUISBOURG AND BOSTON   "   67

V. THE GREAT WEST   "   97

VI. THE VALLEY OF THE OHIO   "   145

VII. THE EXPULSION OF THE ACADIANS   "   164

VIII. THE VICTORIES OF MONTCALM   "   178

IX. MONTCALM AT QUEBEC   "   198

X. THE STRATEGY OF PITT   "   210

XI. THE FALL OF CANADA   "   225

BIBLIOGRAPHICAL NOTE   "   239

INDEX   "   241

ILLUSTRATIONS

THE SIEGE OF LOUISBOURG, 1745
   From the painting by C. W. Jefferys.   *Frontispiece*

MAP TO ILLUSTRATE THE CONQUEST
   OF NEW FRANCE
   Prepared by W. L. G. Joerg, American
   Geographical Society.   *Facing page*   70

THE CONQUEST OF NEW FRANCE

.·.

CHAPTER I

THE CONFLICT OPENS: FRONTENAC AND PHIPS

MANY centuries of European history had been
marked by war almost ceaseless between France
and England when these two states first confronted
each other in America. The conflict for the New
World was but the continuation of an age-long
antagonism in the Old, intensified now by the
savagery of the wilderness and by new dreams of
empire. There was another potent cause of strife
which had not existed in the earlier days. When,
during the fourteenth and fifteenth centuries, the
antagonists had fought through the interminable
Hundred Years' War, they had been of the same
religious faith. Since then, however, England had
become Protestant, while France had remained
Catholic. When the rivals first met on the shores

1

of the New World, colonial America was still very young. It was in 1607 that the English occupied Virginia. At the same time the French were securing a foothold in Acadia, now Nova Scotia. Six years had barely passed when the English Captain Argall sailed to the north from Virginia and destroyed the rising French settlements. Sixteen years after this another English force attacked and captured Quebec. Presently these conquests were restored. France remained in possession of the St. Lawrence and in virtual possession of Acadia. The English colonies, holding a great stretch of the Atlantic seaboard, increased in number and power. New France also grew stronger. The steady hostility of the rivals never wavered. There was, indeed, little open warfare as long as the two Crowns remained at peace. From 1660 to 1688, the Stuart rulers of England remained subservient to their cousin the Bourbon King of France and at one with him in religious faith. But after the fall of the Stuarts France bitterly denounced the new King, William of Orange, as both a heretic and a usurper, and attacked the English in America with a savage fury unknown in Europe. From 1690 to 1760 the combatants fought with little more than pauses for renewed preparation; and the conflict ended only when France yielded to England the mastery of her empire in America. It is the story of this struggle, covering a period of seventy years, which is told in the following pages.

The career of Louis de Buade, Comte de Frontenac, who was Governor of Canada from 1672 to 1682 and again from 1689 to his death in 1698, reveals both the merits and the defects of the colonizing genius of France. Frontenac was a man of noble birth whose life had been spent in court and camp. The story of his family, so far as it is known, is a story of attendance upon the royal house of France. His father and uncles had been playmates of the young Dauphin, afterwards Louis XIII. The thoughts familiar to Frontenac in his youth remained with him through life; and, when he went to rule at Quebec, the very spirit that dominated the court at Versailles crossed the sea with him.

A man is known by the things he loves. The things which Frontenac most highly cherished were marks of royal favor, the ceremony due to his own rank, the right to command. He was an egoist, supremely interested in himself.

He was poor, but at his country seat in France, near Blois, he kept open house in the style of a great noble. Always he bore himself as one to whom much was due. His guests were expected to admire his indifferent horses as the finest to be seen, his gardens as the most beautiful, his clothes as of the most effective cut and finish, the plate on his table as of the best workmanship, and the food as having superior flavor. He scolded his equals as if they were naughty children.

Yet there was genius in this showy court figure. In 1669, when the Venetian Republic had asked France to lend her an efficient soldier to lead against the rampant Turk, the great Marshal Turenne had chosen Frontenac for the task. Crete, which Frontenac was to rescue, the Turk indeed had taken; but, it is said, at the fearful cost of a hundred and eighty thousand men. Three years later, Frontenac had been sent to Canada to war with the savage Iroquois and to hold in check the aggressive designs of the English. He had been recalled in 1682, after ten years of service, chiefly on account of his arbitrary temper. He had quarreled with the Bishop. He had bullied the Intendant until at one time that harried official had barricaded his house and armed his servants.

He had told the Jesuit missionaries that they thought more of selling beaver-skins than of saving souls. He had insulted those about him, sulked, threatened, foamed at the mouth in rage, revealed a childish vanity in regard to his dignity, and a hunger insatiable for marks of honor from the King — "more grateful," he once said, "than anything else to a heart shaped after the right pattern."

France, however, now required at Quebec a man who could do the needed man's tasks. The real worth of Frontenac had been tested; and so, in 1689, when England had driven from her shores her Catholic king and when France's colony across the sea seemed to be in grave danger from the Iroquois allies of the English, Frontenac was sent again to Quebec to subdue these savages and, if he could, to destroy in America the power of the age-long enemy of his country.

Perched high above the St. Lawrence, on a noble site where now is a public terrace and a great hotel, stood the Château St. Louis, the scene of Frontenac's rule as head of the colony. No other spot in the world commanded such a highway linking the inland waters with the sea. The French had always an eye for points of strategic value; and in holding Quebec they hoped to possess the pivot on which the destinies of North America should turn. For a long time it seemed, indeed, as if this glowing vision might become a reality. The imperial ideas which were working at Quebec were based upon the substantial realities of trade. The instinct for business was hardly less strong in these keen adventurers than the instinct for empire. In promise of trade the interior of North America was rich. Today its vast agriculture and its wealth in minerals have brought rewards beyond the dreams of two hundred years ago. The wealth, however, sought by the leaders of that time came from furs. In those wastes of river, lake, and forest were the richest preserves in the world for fur-bearing animals.

This vast wilderness was not an unoccupied land. In those wild regions dwelt many savage tribes. Some of the natives were by no means without political capacity. On the contrary, they were long clever enough to pit English against French to their own advantage as the real sovereigns in North America. One of them, whose fluent oratory had won for him the name of Big Mouth, told the Governor of Canada, in 1688, that his people held their lands from the Great Spirit, that they yielded no lordship to either the English or the French, that they well understood the weakness of the French and were quite able to destroy them, but that they wished to be friends with both French and English who brought to them the advantages of trade. In sagacity of council and dignity of carriage some of these Indians so bore themselves that to trained observers they seemed not unequal to the diplomats of Europe. They were, however, weak before the superior knowledge of the white men. In all their long centuries in America they had learned nothing of the use of iron. Their sharpest tool had been made of chipped obsidian or of hammered copper. Their most potent weapons had been the stone hatchet or axe and the bow and arrow. It thus happened that, when steel and gunpowder reached America, the natives soon came to despise their primitive implements. More and more they craved the supplies from Europe which multiplied in a hundred ways their strength in the conflict with nature and with man. To the Indian tribes trade with the French or English soon became a vital necessity. From the far northwest for a thousand miles to the bleak shores of Hudson Bay, from the banks of the Mississippi to the banks of the St. Lawrence and the Hudson, they came each year on laborious journeys, paddling their canoes and carrying them over portages, to barter furs for the things which they must have and which the white man alone could supply.

The Iroquois, the ablest and most resolute of the native tribes, held the lands bordering on Lake Ontario which commanded the approaches from both the Hudson and the St. Lawrence by the Great Lakes to the spacious regions of the West. The five tribes known as the Iroquois had shown marked political talent by forming themselves into a confederacy. From the time of Champlain, the founder of Quebec, there had been trouble between the French and the Iroquois. In spite of this bad beginning, the French had later done their best to make friends with the powerful confederacy. They had sent to them devoted missionaries, many of whom met the martyr's reward of torture and massacre. But the opposing influence of the English, with whom the Iroquois chiefly traded, proved too strong.

With the Iroquois hostile, it was too dangerous for the French to travel inland by way of Lake Ontario. They had, it is true, a shorter and, indeed, a better route farther north, by way of the Ottawa River and Lake Nipissing to Lake Huron. In time, however, the Iroquois made even this route unsafe. Their power was far-reaching and their ambition limitless. They aimed to be masters of North America. Like all virile but backward peoples, they believed themselves superior to every other race. Their orators declared that the fate of the world was to turn on their policy.

On Frontenac's return to Canada he had a stormy inheritance in confronting the Iroquois. They had real grievances against France. Denonville, Frontenac's predecessor, had met their treachery by treachery of his own. Louis XIV had found that these lusty savages made excellent galley slaves and had ordered Denonville to secure a supply in Canada. In consequence the Frenchman seized even friendly Iroquois and sent them over seas to France. The savages in retaliation exacted a fearful vengeance in the butchery of French colonists. The bloodiest story in the annals of Canada is the massacre at Lachine, a village a few miles above Montreal. On the night of August 4, 1689, fourteen hundred Iroquois burst in on the village and a wild orgy of massacre followed. All Canada was in a panic. Some weeks later Frontenac arrived at Quebec and took command.

To the old soldier, now in his seventieth year, his hard task was not uncongenial. He had fought the savage Iroquois before and the no less savage Turk. He belonged to that school of military action which knows no scruple in its methods, and he was prepared to make war with all the frightfulness practised by the savages themselves. His resolute, blustering demeanor was well fitted to impress the red men of the forest, for an imperious eye will sometimes cow an Indian as well as a lion, and Frontenac's mien was imperious. In his life in court and camp he had learned how to command.

The English in New York had professed to be brothers to the Iroquois and had called them by that name. This title of equality, however, Frontenac would not yield. Kings speak of "my people"; Frontenac spoke to the Indians not as his brothers but as his children and as children of the great King whom he served. He was their father, their protector, the disposer and controller of mighty reserves of power, who loved and cared for those putting their trust in him. He could unbend to play with their children and give presents to their squaws. At times he seemed patient, gentle, and forgiving. At times, too, he swaggered and boasted in terms which the event did not always justify.

La Potherie, a cultivated Frenchman in Canada during Frontenac's régime, describes an amazing scene at Montreal, which seems to show that, whether Frontenac recognized the title or not, he had qualities which made him the real brother of the savages. In 1690 Huron and other Indian allies of the French had come from the far interior to trade and also to consider the eternal question of checking the Iroquois. At the council, which began with grave decorum, a Huron orator begged the French to make no terms with the Iroquois. Frontenac answered in the high tone which he could so well assume. He would fight them until they should humbly crave peace; he would make with them no treaty except in concert with his Indian allies, whom he would never fail in fatherly care. To impress the council by the reality of his oneness with the Indians, Frontenac now seized a tomahawk and brandished it in the air shouting at the same time the Indian war-song. The whole assembly, French and Indians, joined in a wild orgy of war passion, and the old man of seventy, fresh from the court of Louis XIV, led in the war-dance, yelled with the Indians their savage war-whoops, danced round the circle of the council, and showed himself in spirit a brother of the wildest of them. This was good diplomacy. The savages swore to make war to the end under his lead. Many a frontier outrage, many a village attacked in the dead of night and burned, amidst bloody massacre of its few toil-worn settlers, was to be the result of that strange mingling of Europe with wild America.

Frontenac's task was to make war on the English and their Iroquois allies. He had before him the King's instructions as to the means for effecting this. The King aimed at nothing less than the conquest of the English colonies in America. In 1664 the English, by a sudden blow in time of peace, had captured New Netherland, the Dutch colony on the Hudson, which then became New York. Now, a quarter of a century later, France thought to strike a similar blow against the English, and Louis XIV was resolved that the conquest should be thoroughgoing. The Dutch power had fallen before a meager naval force. The English now would have to face one much more formidable. Two French ships were to cross the sea and to lie in wait near New York. Meanwhile from Canada, sixteen hundred armed men, a thousand of them French regular troops, were to advance by land into the heart of the colony, seize Albany and all the boats there available, and descend by the Hudson to New York. The warships, hovering off the coast, would then enter New York harbor at the same time that the land forces made their attack. The village, for it was hardly more than this, contained, as the French believed, only some two hundred houses and four hundred fighting men and it was thought that a month would suffice to complete this whole work of conquest. Once victors, the French were to show no pity. All private property, but that of Catholics, was to be confiscated. Catholics, whether English or Dutch, were to be left undisturbed if not too numerous and if they would take the oath of allegiance to Louis XIV and show some promise of keeping it. Rich Protestants were to be held for ransom. All the other inhabitants, except those whom the French might find useful for their own purposes, were to be driven out of the colony, homeless wanderers, to be scattered far so that they could not combine to recover what they had lost. With New York taken, New England would be so weakened that in time it too would fall. Such was the plan of conquest which came from the brilliant chambers at Versailles.

New York did not fall. The expedition so

carefully planned came to nothing. Frontenac had never shown much faith in the enterprise. At Quebec, on his arrival in the autumn of 1689, he was planning something less ideally perfect, but certain to produce results. The scarred old courtier intended so to terrorize the English that they should make no aggressive advance, to encourage the French to believe themselves superior to their rivals, and, above all, to prove to the Indian tribes that prudence dictated alliance with the French and not with the English.

Frontenac wrote a tale of blood. There were three war parties; one set out from Montreal against New York, and one from Three Rivers and one from Quebec against the frontier settlements of New Hampshire and Maine. To describe one is to describe all. A band of one hundred and sixty Frenchmen, with nearly as many Indians, gathers at Montreal in mid-winter. The ground is deep with snow and they troop on snowshoes across the white wastes. Dragging on sleds the needed supplies, they march up the Richelieu River and over the frozen surface of Lake Champlain. As they advance with caution into the colony of New York they suffer terribly, now from bitter cold, now from thaws which make the soft trail almost impassable. On a February night their scouts tell them that they are near Schenectady, on the English frontier. There are young members of the Canadian *noblesse* in the party. In the dead of night they creep up to the paling which surrounds the village. The signal is given and the village is awakened by the terrible war-whoop. Doors are smashed by axes and hatchets, and women and children are killed as they lie in bed, or kneel, shrieking for mercy. Houses are set on fire and living human beings are thrown into the flames. By midday the assailants have finished their dread work and are retreating along the forest paths dragging with them a few miserable captives. In this winter of 1689–90 raiding parties also came back from the borders of New Hampshire and of Maine with news of similar exploits, and Quebec and Montreal glowed with the joy of victory.

Far away an answering attack was soon on foot. Sir William Phips of Massachusetts, the son of a poor settler on the Kennebec River, had made his first advance in life by taking up the trade of carpenter in Boston. Only when grown up had he learned to read and write. He married a rich wife, and ease of circumstances freed his mind for great designs. Some fifty years before he was thus relieved of material cares, a Spanish galleon carrying vast wealth had been wrecked in the West Indies. Phips now planned to raise the ship and get the money. For this enterprise he obtained support in England and set out on his exacting adventure. On the voyage his crew mutinied. Armed with cutlasses, they told Phips that he must turn pirate or perish; but he attacked the leader with his fists and triumphed by sheer strength of body and will. A second mutiny he also quelled, and then took his ship to Jamaica where he got rid of its worthless crew. His enterprise had apparently failed; but the second Duke of Albemarle and other powerful men believed in him and helped him to make another trial. This time he succeeded in finding the wreck on the coast of Hispaniola, and took possession of its cargo of precious metals and jewels — treasure to the value of three hundred thousand pounds sterling. Of the spoil Phips himself received sixteen thousand pounds, a great fortune for a New Englander in those days. He was also knighted for his services and, in the end, was named by William and Mary the first royal Governor of Massachusetts.

Massachusetts, whose people had been thoroughly aroused by the French incursions, resolved to retaliate by striking at the heart of Canada by sea and to take Quebec. Sir William Phips, though not yet made Governor, would lead the expedition. The first blow fell in Acadia. Phips sailed up the Bay of Fundy and on May 11, 1690, landed a force before Port Royal. The French Governor surrendered on terms. The conquest was intended to be final, and the people were offered their lives and property on the condition of taking the oath to be loyal subjects of William and Mary. This many of them did and were left unmolested. It was a bloodless victory. But Phips, the Puritan crusader, was something of a pirate. He plundered private property and was himself accused of taking not merely the silver forks and spoons of the captive Governor but even his wigs, shirts, garters, and night caps. The Boston Puritans joyfully pillaged the church at Port Royal, and overturned the high altar and the images. The booty was considerable and by the end of May Phips, a prosperous hero, was back in Boston.

Boston was aflame with zeal to go on and conquer Canada. By the middle of August Phips had set out on the long sea voyage to Quebec, with twenty-two hundred men, a great force for a colonial enterprise of that time, and in all some forty ships. The voyage occupied more than two months. Apparently the hardy carpenter-sailor, able enough to carry through a difficult undertaking with a single ship, lacked the organizing skill to manage a great expedition. He performed, however, the feat of navigating safely with his fleet the treacherous waters of the lower St. Lawrence. On the morning of October 16, 1690, watchers at Quebec saw the fleet, concerning which they had already been warned, rounding the head of the Island of Orleans and sailing into the broad basin. Breathless spectators counted the ships. There were thirty-four in sight, a few large vessels, some mere fishing craft. It was a spectacle well calculated to excite and alarm the good people of Quebec. They might, however, take comfort in the knowledge that their great Frontenac was present to defend them. A few days earlier he had been in Montreal, but, when there had come the startling news of the approach of the enemy's ships, he had hurried down the river and had been received with shouts of joy by the anxious populace.

The situation was one well suited to Frontenac's

genius for the dramatic. When a boat under a flag of truce put out from the English ships, Frontenac hurried four canoes to meet it. The English envoy was placed blindfold in one of these canoes and was paddled to the shore. Here two soldiers took him by the arms and led him over many obstacles up the steep ascent to the Château St. Louis. He could see nothing but could hear the beating of drums, the blowing of trumpets, the jeers and shouting of a great multitude in a town which seemed to be full of soldiers and to have its streets heavily barricaded. When the bandage was taken from his eyes he found himself in a great room of the Château. Before him stood Frontenac, in brilliant uniform, surrounded by the most glittering array of officers which Quebec could muster. The astonished envoy presented a letter from Phips. It was a curt demand in the name of King William of England for the unconditional surrender of all "forts and castles" in Canada, of Frontenac himself, and all his forces and supplies. On such conditions Phips would show mercy, as a Christian should. Frontenac must answer within an hour. When the letter had been read the envoy took a watch from his pocket and pointed out the time to Frontenac. It was ten o'clock. The reply must be given by eleven. Loud mutterings greeted the insulting message. One officer cried out that Phips was a pirate and that his messenger should be hanged. Frontenac knew well how to deal with such a situation. He threw the letter in the envoy's face and turned his back upon him. The unhappy man, who understood French, heard the Governor give orders that a gibbet should be erected on which he was to be hanged. When the Bishop and the Intendant pleaded for mercy, Frontenac seemed to yield. He would not take, he said, an hour to reply, but would answer at once. He knew no such person as King William. James, though in exile, was the true King of England and the good friend of the King of France. There would be no surrender to a pirate. After this outburst, the envoy asked if he might have the answer in writing. "No!" thundered Frontenac. "I will answer only from the mouths of my cannon and with my musketry!"

Phips could not take Quebec. In carrying out his plans, he was slow and dilatory. Nature aided his foe. The weather was bad, the waters before Quebec were difficult, and boats grounded unexpectedly in a falling tide. Phips landed a force on the north side of the basin at Beauport but was held in check by French and Indian skirmishing parties. He sailed his ships up close to Quebec and bombarded the stronghold, but then, as now, ships were impotent against well-served land defenses. Soon Phips was short of ammunition. A second time he made a landing in order to attack Quebec from the valley of the St. Charles but French regulars fought with militia and Indians to drive off his forces. Phips held a meeting with his officers for prayer. Heaven, however, denied success to his arms. If he could not take Quebec, it was time to be gone, for in the late autumn the dangers of the St. Lawrence are great. He lay before Quebec for just a week and on the 23d of October sailed away. It was late in November when his battered fleet began to straggle into Boston. The ways of God had not proved as simple as they had seemed to the Puritan faith, for the stronghold of Satan had not fallen before the attacks of the Lord's people. There were searchings of heart, recriminations, and financial distress in Boston.

For seven years more the war endured. Frontenac's victory over Phips at Quebec was not victory over the Iroquois or victory over the colony of New York. In 1691 this colony sent Peter

Schuyler with a force against Canada by way of Lake Champlain. Schuyler penetrated almost to Montreal, gained some indecisive success, and caused much suffering to the unhappy Canadian settlers. Frontenac made his last great stroke in July, 1696, when he led more than two thousand men through the primeval forest to destroy the villages of the Onondaga and the Oneida tribes of the Iroquois. On the journey from the south shore of Lake Ontario, the old man of seventy-five was unable to walk over the rough portages and fifty Indians shouting songs of joy carried his great canoe on their shoulders. When the soldiers left the canoes and marched forward to the fight, they bore Frontenac in an easy chair. He did not destroy his enemy, for many of the Indians fled, but he burned their chief village and taught them a new respect for the power of the French. It was the last great effort of the old warrior. In the next year, 1697, was concluded the Peace of Ryswick; and in 1698 Frontenac died in his seventy-ninth year, a hoary champion of France's imperial designs.

The Peace of Ryswick was an indecisive ending of an indecisive war. It was indeed one of those bad treaties which invite renewed war. The struggle had achieved little but to deepen the conviction of each side that it must make itself stronger for the next fight. Each gave back most of what it had gained. The peace, however, did not leave matters quite as they had been. The position of William was stronger than before, for France had treated with him and now recognized him as King of England. Moreover France, hitherto always victorious, with generals who had not known defeat, was really defeated when she could not longer advance.

CHAPTER II

QUEBEC AND BOSTON

AT the end of the seventeenth century it must have seemed a far cry from Versailles to Quebec. The ocean was crossed only by small sailing vessels haunted by both tempest and pestilence, the one likely to prolong the voyage by many weeks, the other to involve the sacrifice of scores of lives through scurvy and other maladies. Yet, remote as the colony seemed, Quebec was the child of Versailles, protected and nourished by Louis XIV and directed by him in its minutest affairs. The King spent laborious hours over papers relating to the cherished colony across the sea. He sent wise counsel to his officials in Canada and with tactful patience rebuked their faults. He did everything for the colonists — gave them not merely land, but muskets, farm implements, even chickens, pigs, and sometimes wives. The defect of his government was that it tended to be too paternal.

The vital needs of a colony struggling with the problems of barbarism could hardly be read correctly and provided for at Versailles. Colonies, like men, are strong only when they learn to take care of themselves.

The English colonies present a vivid contrast. London did not direct and control Boston. In London the will, indeed, was not wanting, for the Stuart kings, Charles II and James II, were not less despotic in spirit than Louis XIV. But while in France there was a vast organism which moved only as the King willed, in England power was more widely distributed. It may be claimed with truth that English national liberties are a growth from the local freedom which has existed from time immemorial. When British colonists left the motherland to found a new society, their first instinct was to create institutions which involved local control. The solemn covenant by which in 1620 the worn company of the *Mayflower*, after a long and painful voyage, pledged themselves to create a self-governing society, was the inevitable expression of the English political spirit. Do what it would, London could never control Boston as Versailles controlled Quebec.

The English colonist kept his eyes fixed on his

own fortunes.   From the state he expected little; from himself, everything.   He had no great sense of unity with neighboring colonists under the same crown.   Only when he realized some peril to his interests, some menace which would master him if he did not fight, was he stirred to warlike energy. French leaders, on the other hand, were thinking of world politics.   The voyage of Verrazano, the Italian sailor who had been sent out by Francis I of France in 1524, and who had sailed along a great stretch of the Atlantic coast, was deemed by Frenchmen a sufficient title to the whole of North America.   They flouted England's claim based upon the voyages of the Cabots nearly thirty years earlier.   Spain, indeed, might claim Florida, but the English had no real right to any footing in the New World.   As late as in 1720, when the fortunes of France were already on the wane in the New World, Father Bobé, a priest of the Congregation of Missions, presented to the French court a document which sets forth in uncompromising terms the rights of France to all the land between the thirtieth and the fiftieth parallels of latitude. True, he says, others occupy much of this territory, but France must drive out intruders and in particular the English.   Boston rightly belongs to France and so also do New York and Philadelphia. The only regions to which England has any just claim are Acadia, Newfoundland, and Hudson Bay, ceded by France under the Treaty of Utrecht in 1713. This weak cession all true Frenchmen regret and England must hand the territories back. She owes France compensation for her long occupation of lands not really hers. If she makes immediate restitution, the King of France, generous and kind, will forego some of his rights and allow England to retain a strip some fifty miles wide extending from Maine to Florida. France has the right to the whole of the interior. In the mind of the reverend memorialist, no doubt, there was the conviction that England would soon lose the meager strip, fifty miles wide, which France might yield.

These dreams of power had a certain substance. It seems to us now that, from the first, the French were dreaming of the impossible. We know what has happened, and after the event it is an easy task to measure political forces. The ambitions of France were not, however, empty fancies. More than once she has seemed on the point of mastering the nations of the West. Just before the year 1690 she had a great opportunity. In

England, in 1660, the fall of the system created by Oliver Cromwell brought back to the English throne the House of Stuart, for centuries the ally and usually the pupil of France. Stuart kings of Scotland, allied with France, had fought the Tudor kings of England. Stuarts in misfortune had been the pensioners of France. Charles II, a Stuart, alien in religion to the convictions of his people, looked to Catholic France to give him security on his throne. Before the first half of the reign of Louis XIV had ended, it was the boast of the French that the King of England was vassal to their King, that the states of continental Europe had become mere pawns in the game of their Grand Monarch, and that France could be master of as much of the world as was really worth mastering. In 1679 the Canadian Intendant, Duchesneau, writing from Quebec to complain of the despotic conduct of the Governor, Frontenac, paid a tribute to "the King our master, of whom the whole world stands in awe, who has just given law to all Europe."

To men thus obsessed by the greatness of their own ruler it seemed no impossible task to overthrow a few English colonies in America of whose King their own was the patron and the paymaster.

The world of high politics has never been conspicuous for its knowledge of human nature. A strong blow from a strong arm would, it was believed both at Versailles and Quebec, shatter forever a weak rival and give France the prize of North America. Officers in Canada talked loftily of the ease with which France might master all the English colonies. The Canadians, it was said, were a brave and warlike people, trained to endure hardship, while the English colonists were undisciplined, ignorant of war, and cowardly. The link between them and the motherland, said these observers, could be easily broken, for the colonies were longing to be free. There is no doubt that France could put into the field armies vastly greater than those of England. Had the French been able to cross the Channel, march on London and destroy English power at its root, the story of civilization in a great part of North America might well have been different, and we should perhaps find now on the banks of the Hudson what we find on the banks of the St. Lawrence — villages dominated by great churches and convents, with inhabitants Catholic to a man, speaking the language and preserving the traditions of France. The strip of inviolate sea between Calais and

Dover made impossible, however, an assault on London. Sea power kept secure not only England but English effort in America and in the end defeated France.

England had defenses other than her great strength on the sea. In spite of the docility towards France shown by the English King, Charles II, himself half French in blood and at heart devoted to the triumph of the Catholic faith, the English people would tolerate no policies likely to make England subservient to France. This was forbidden by age-long tradition. The struggle had become one of religion as well as of race. A fight for a century and a half with the Roman Catholic Church had made England sternly, fanatically Protestant. In their suspicion of the system which France accepted, Englishmen had sent a king to the scaffold, had overthrown the monarchy, and had created a military republic. This republic, indeed, had fallen, but the distrust of the aims of the Roman Catholic Church remained intense and burst into passionate fury the moment an understanding of the aims of France gained currency.

There are indeed few passages in English history less creditable than the panic fear of Roman Catholic plots which swept the country in the days when Frontenac at Quebec was working to destroy English and Protestant influence in America. In 1678, Titus Oates, a clergyman of the Church of England who had turned Roman Catholic, declared that, while in the secrets of his new church, he had found on foot a plot to restore Roman Catholic dominance in England by means of the murder of Charles II and of any other crimes necessary for that purpose. Oates said that he had left the Church and returned to his former faith because of the terrible character of the conspiracy which he had discovered. His story was not even plausible; he was known to be a man of vicious life; moreover, Catholic plotters would hardly murder a king who was at heart devoted to Catholic policy. England, however, was in a nervous state of mind; Charles II was known to be intriguing with France; and a cruel fury surged through the nation. For a share in the supposed plots a score of people, among them one of the great nobles of England, the venerable and innocent Earl of Stafford, were condemned to death and executed. Whatever Charles II himself might have thought, he was obliged for his own safety to acquiesce in the policy of persecution.

Catholic France was not less malignant than Protestant England. Though cruel severity had long been shown to Protestants, they seemed to be secure under the law of France in certain limited rights and in a restricted toleration. In 1685, however, Louis XIV revoked the Edict of Nantes by which Henry IV a century earlier had guaranteed this toleration. All over France there had already burst out terrible persecution, and the act of Louis XIV brought a fiery climax. Unhappy heretics who would not accept Roman Catholic doctrine found life intolerable. Tens of thousands escaped from France in spite of a law which, though it exiled the Protestant ministers, forbade other Protestants to leave the country. Stories of plots were made the excuse to seize the property of Protestants. Regiments of soldiers, charged with the task, could boast of many enforced "conversions." Quartered on Protestant households, they made the life of the inmates a burden until they abandoned their religion. Among the means used were torture before a slow fire, the tearing off of the finger nails, the driving of the whole families naked into the streets and the forbidding of any one to give them shelter, the violation of women, and the crowding of the heretics in loathsome prisons. By such means it took a regiment of soldiers in Rouen only a few days to "convert" to the old faith some six hundred families. Protestant ministers caught in France were sent to the galleys for life. The persecutions which followed the revocation of the Edict of Nantes outdid even Titus Oates.

Charles II died in 1685 and the scene at his deathbed encouraged in England suspicions of Catholic policy and in France hope that this policy was near its climax of success. Though indolent and dissolute, Charles yet possessed striking mental capacity and insight. He knew well that to preserve his throne he must remain outwardly a Protestant and must also respect the liberties of the English nation. He cherished, however, the Roman Catholic faith and the despotic ideals of his Bourbon mother. On his deathbed he avowed his real belief. With great precautions for secrecy, he was received into the Roman Catholic Church and comforted with the consolations which it offers to the dying. While this secret was suspected by the English people, one further fact was perfectly clear. Their new King, James II, was a zealous Roman Catholic, who would use all his influence to bring England back

3

to the Roman communion. Suspicion of the King's designs soon became certainty and, after four years of bitter conflict with James, the inevitable happened. The Roman Catholic Stuart King was driven from his throne and his daughter Mary and her Protestant husband, William of Orange, became the sovereigns of England by choice of the English Parliament. Again had the struggle between Roman Catholic and Protestant brought revolution in England, and the politics of Europe dominated America. The revolution in London was followed by revolution in Boston and New York. The authority of James II was repudiated. His chief agent in New England, Sir Edmund Andros, was seized and imprisoned, and William and Mary reigned over the English colonies in America as they reigned over the motherland.

To the loyal Catholics of France the English, who had driven out a Catholic king and dethroned an ancient line, were guilty of the double sin of heresy and of treason. To the Jesuit enthusiast in Canada not only were they infidel devils in human shape upon whose plans must rest the curse of God; they were also rebels, republican successors of the accursed Cromwell, who had sent an anointed king to the block. It would be a holy thing to destroy this lawless power which ruled from London. The Puritans of Boston were, in turn, not less convinced that theirs was the cause of God, and that Satan, enthroned in the French dominance at Quebec, must soon fall. The smaller the pit the fiercer the rats. Passions raged in the petty colonial capitals more bitterly than even in London and Paris. This intensity of religious differences embittered the struggle for the mastery of the new continent.

The English colonies had twenty white men to one in Canada. Yet Canada was long able to wage war on something like equal terms. She had the supreme advantage of a single control. There was no trouble at Quebec about getting a reluctant legislature to vote money for war purposes. No semblance of an elected legislature existed and the money for war came not from the Canadians, but from the capacious, if now usually depleted, coffers of the French court at Versailles. In the English colonies the legislatures preferred, of all political struggles, one about money with the Governor, the representative of the King. At least one of the English colonies, Pennsylvania, believing that evil is best conquered by non-resistance, was resolutely against war for any reason, good or bad. Other colonies often raised the more sordid objection that they were too poor to help in war. The colonial legislatures, indeed, with their eternal demand for the privileges and rights which the British House of Commons had won in the long centuries of its history, constitute the most striking of all the contrasts with Canada. In them were always the sparks of an independent temper. The English diarist, Evelyn, wrote, in 1671, that New England was in "a peevish and touchy humour." Colonists who go out to found a new state will always demand rights like those which they have enjoyed at home. It was unthinkable that men of Boston, who, themselves, or whose party in England, had fought against a despotic king, had sent him to the block and driven his son from the throne, would be content with anything short of controlling the taxes which they paid, making the laws which they obeyed, and carrying on their affairs in their own way. When obliged to accept a governor from England, they were resolved as far as possible to remain his paymaster. In a majority of the colonies they insisted that the salary of the Governor should be voted each year by their representatives, in order that

they might be able always to use against him the co-
gent logic of financial need. On questions of this
kind Quebec had nothing to say. To the King
in France and to him alone went all demands for
pay and honors. If, in such things, the people of
Canada had no remote voice, they were still as
well off as Frenchmen in France. New England
was a copy of Old England and New France a
copy of Old France. There was, as yet, no "peevish and touchy humour" at either Quebec or Versailles in respect to political rights.

Canada, in spite of its scanty population, was
better equipped for war than was any of the English colonies. The French were largely explorers
and hunters, familiar with hardship and danger
and led by men with a love of adventure. The
English, on the other hand, were chiefly traders
and farmers who disliked and dreaded the horrors
of war. There was not to be found in all the
English colonies a family of the type of the Canadian family of Le Moyne. Charles Le Moyne,
of Montreal, a member of the Canadian *noblesse*,
had ten sons, every one of whom showed the spirit
and capacity of the adventurous soldier. They
all served in the time of Frontenac. The most
famous of them, Pierre Le Moyne d'Iberville,

shines in varied rôles. He was a frontier leader
who made his name a terror in the English settlements; a sailor who seized and ravaged the English
settlements in Newfoundland, who led a French
squadron to the remote and chill waters of Hudson Bay, and captured there the English strong-
holds of the fur trade; and a leader in the more
peaceful task of founding, at the mouth of the
Mississippi, the colony of Louisiana. Canada had
the advantage over the English colonies in bold
pioneers of this type.

Canada was never doubtful of the English peril
or divided in the desire to destroy it. Nearly
always, a soldier or a naval officer ruled in the
Château St. Louis, at Quebec, with eyes alert to see
and arms ready to avert military danger. England sometimes sent to her colonies in America
governors who were disreputable and inefficient,
needy hangers-on, too well-known at home to make
it wise there to give them office, but thought good
enough for the colonies. It would not have been
easy to find a governor less fitted to maintain the
dignity and culture of high office than Sir William
Phips, Governor of Massachusetts in the time
of Frontenac. Phips, however, though a rough
brawler, was reasonably efficient, but Lord Corn-

bury, who became Earl of Clarendon, owed his appointment as Governor of New Jersey and New York in 1701, only to his necessities and to the desire of his powerful connections to provide for him. Queen Anne was his cousin. He was a profligate, feeble in mind but arrogant in spirit, with no burden of honesty and a great burden of debt, and he made no change in his scandalous mode of life when he represented his sovereign at New York. There were other governors only slightly better. Canada had none as bad. Her viceroys as a rule kept up the dignity of their office and respected the decencies of life. In English colonies, governors eked out their incomes by charging heavy fees for official acts and any one who refused to pay such fees was not likely to secure attention to his business. In Canada the population was too scanty and the opportunity too limited to furnish happy hunting-grounds of this kind. The governors, however, badly paid as they were, must live, and, in the case of a man like Frontenac, repair fortunes shattered at court. To do so they were likely to have some concealed interest in the fur trade. This was forbidden by the court but was almost a universal practice. Some of the governors carried trading to great lengths and aroused the bitter hostility of rival trading interests. The fur trade was easily controlled as a government monopoly and it was unfair that a needy governor should share its profits. But, after all, such a quarrel was only between rival monopolists. Better a trading governor than one who plundered the people or who by drunken profligacy discredited his office.

While all Canada was devoted to the Roman Catholic Church, the diversity of religious beliefs in the English colonies was a marked feature of social life. In Virginia, by law of the colony, the Church of England was the established Church. In Massachusetts, founded by stern Puritans, the public services of the Church of England were long prohibited. In Pennsylvania there was dominant the sect derisively called "Quakers," who would have no ecclesiastical organization and believed that religion was purely a matter for the individual soul. Boston jeered at the superstitions of Quebec, such as the belief of the missionaries that a drop of water, with the murmured words of baptism, transformed a dying Indian child from an outcast savage into an angel of light. Quebec might, however, deride Boston with equal justice.

Sir William Phips believed that malignant and invisible devils had made a special invasion of Massachusetts, dragging people from their houses, pushing them into fire and water, and carrying them through the air for miles over trees and hills. These devils, it was thought, took visible form, of which the favorite was that of a black cat. Witches were thought to be able to pass through keyholes and to exercise charms which would destroy their victims. While Phips and Frontenac were struggling for the mastery of Canada, a fever of excitement ran through New England about these perils of witchcraft. When, in 1692, Phips became Governor of Massachusetts, he named a special court to try accused persons. The court considered hundreds of cases and condemned and hanged nineteen persons for wholly imaginary crimes. Whatever the faults of the rule of the priests at Quebec, they never equaled this in brutality or surpassed it in blind superstition. In New England we find bitter religious persecution. In Canada there was none: the door was completely closed to Protestants and the family within were all of one mind. There was no one to persecute.

The old contrast between French and English

ideals still endures.   At Quebec there was an early zeal for education.   In 1638, the year in which Harvard College was organized, a college and a school for training the French youth and the natives were founded at Quebec.   In the next year the Ursuline nuns established at Quebec the convent which through all the intervening years has continued its important work of educating girls.   In zeal for education Quebec was therefore not behind Boston.   But the spirit was different. Quebec believed that safety lay in control by the Church, and this control it still maintains.   Massachusetts came in time to believe that safety lay in freeing education from any spiritual authority. Today Laval University at Quebec and Harvard University at Cambridge represent the outcome of these differing modes of thought.   Other forces were working to produce essentially different types. The printing-press Quebec did not know; and, down to the final overthrow of the French power in 1763, no newspaper or book was issued in Canada.   Massachusetts, on the other hand, had a printing-press as early as in 1638 and soon books were being printed in the colony.   Of course, in the spirit of the time, there was a strict censorship.   But, by 1722, this had come to an end, and after that the newspaper, unknown in Canada, was busy and free in its task of helping to mold the thought of the English colonies in America.

CHAPTER III

FRANCE LOSES ACADIA

THE Peace of Ryswick in 1697 had settled nothing finally. France was still strong enough to aim at the mastery of Europe and America. England was torn by internal faction and would not prepare to face her menacing enemy. Always the English have disliked a great standing army. Now, despite the entreaties of a king who knew the real danger, they reduced the army to the pitiable number of seven thousand men. Louis XIV grew ever more confident. In 1700 he was able to put his own grandson on the throne of Spain and to dominate Europe from the Straits of Gibraltar to the Netherlands. Another event showing his resolve soon startled the world. In 1701 died James II, the dethroned King of England, and Louis went out of his way to insult the English people. William III was King by the will of Parliament. Louis had recognized him as such.

Yet, on the death of James, Louis declared that James's son was now the true King of England. This impudent defiance meant, and Louis intended that it should mean, renewed war. England had invited it by making her forces weak. William III died in 1702 and the war went on under his successor, Queen Anne.

Thus it happened that once more war-parties began to prowl on the Canadian frontier, and women and children in remote clearings in the forest shivered at the prospect of the savage scourge. The English colonies suffered terribly. Everywhere France was aggressive. The warlike Iroquois were now so alarmed by the French menace that, to secure protection, they ceded their territory to Queen Anne and became British subjects, a humiliating step indeed for a people who had once thought themselves the most important in all the world. By 1703 the butchery on the frontier was in full operation. The Jesuit historian Charlevoix, with complacent exaggeration, says that in that year alone three hundred men were killed on the New England frontier by the Abenaki Indians incited by the French. The numbers slain were in fact fewer and the slain were not always men but sometimes old women and young babies. The policy of France was to make the war so ruthless that a gulf of hatred should keep their Indian allies from ever making friends and resuming trade with the English, whose hatchets, blankets, and other supplies were, as the French well knew, better and cheaper than their own. The French hoped to seize Boston, to destroy its industries and sink its ships, then to advance beyond Boston and deal out to other places the same fate. The rivalry of New England was to be ended by making that region a desert.

The first fury of the war raged on the frontier of Maine, which was an outpost of Massachusetts. On an August day in 1703 the people of the rugged little settlement of Wells were at their usual tasks when they heard gunshots and war-whoops. Indians had crept up to attack the place. They set the village on fire and killed or carried off some twoscore prisoners, chiefly women and children. The village of Deerfield, on the northwestern frontier of Massachusetts, consisted of a wooden meeting-house and a number of rough cabins which lodged the two or three hundred inhabitants. On a February night in 1704 savages led by a young member of the Canadian *noblesse*, Hertel de Rouville, approached the village silently on snowshoes, waited on the outskirts during the dead of night, and then just before dawn burst in upon the sleeping people. The work was done quickly. Within an hour after dawn the place had been plundered and set on fire, forty or fifty dead bodies of men and women and children lay in the village, and a hundred and eleven miserable prisoners were following their captors on snowshoes through the forest, each prisoner well knowing that to fall by the way meant to have his head split by a tomahawk and the scalp torn off. When on the first night one of them slipped away, Rouville told the others that, should a further escape occur, he would burn alive all those remaining in his hands. The minister of the church at Deerfield, the Reverend John Williams, was a captive, together with his wife and five children. The wife, falling by the way, was killed by a stroke of a tomahawk and the body was left lying on the snow. The children were taken from their father and scattered among different bands. After a tramp of two hundred miles through the wilderness to the outlying Canadian settlements, the minister in the end reached Quebec. Every effort was made, even by his Indian guard, to make him accept the

Roman Catholic faith, but the stern Puritan was obdurate. His daughter, Eunice, on the other hand, caught young, became a Catholic so devoted that later she would not return to New England lest the contact with Protestants should injure her faith. She married a Caughnawaga Indian and became to all outward appearance a squaw. Williams himself lived to resume his career in New England and to write the story of the raid at Deerfield.

It may be that there were men in New England and New York capable of similar barbarities. It is true that the savage allies of the English, when at their worst, knew no restraint. There is nothing in the French raids on a scale as great as that of the murderous raid by the Iroquois on the French village of Lachine. But the Puritans of New England, while they were ready to hew down savages, did not like and rarely took part in the massacre of Europeans.

As the outrages went on year after year the temper of New England towards the savages grew more ruthless. The General Court, the Legislature of Massachusetts, offered forty pounds for every Indian scalp brought in. Indians, like wolves, were vermin to be destroyed. The anger of New England was further kindled by what was happening on the sea. Privateers from Port Royal, in Acadia, attacked New England commerce and New England fishermen and made unsafe the approaches to Boston. This was to touch a commercial community on its most tender spot; and a deep resolve was formed that Canada should be conquered and the menace ended once for all.

It was only an occasional spirit in Massachusetts who made comprehensive political plans. One of these was Samuel Vetch, a man somewhat different from the usual type of New England leader, for he was not of English but of Scottish origin, of the Covenanter strain. Vetch, himself an adventurous trader, had taken a leading part in the ill-fated Scottish attempt to found on the Isthmus of Panama a colony, which, in easy touch with both the Pacific and the Atlantic, should carry on a gigantic commerce between the East and the West. The colony failed, chiefly, perhaps, because Spain would not have this intrusion into territory which she claimed. Tropical disease and the disunion and incompetence of the colonists themselves were Spain's allies in the destruction. After this, Vetch had found his way to Boston, where he soon became prominent. In 1707 Scotland and Eng-

4

land were united under one Parliament, and the active mind of Vetch was occupied with something greater than a Scottish colony at Panama. Queen Anne, Vetch was resolved, should be "Sole Empress of the vast North American Continent." Massachusetts was ready for just such a cry. The General Court took up eagerly the plan of Vetch. The scheme required help from England and the other colonies. To England Vetch went in 1708. Marlborough had just won the great victory of Oudenarde. It was good, the English ministry thought, to hit France wherever she raised her head. In the spring of 1709 Vetch returned to Boston with promises of powerful help at once for an attack on Canada, and with the further promise that, the victory won, he himself should be the first British Governor of Canada. New York was to help with nine hundred men. Other remoter colonies were to aid on a smaller scale. These contingents were to attack Canada by way of Lake Champlain. Twelve hundred men from New England were to join the regulars from England and go against Quebec by way of the sea and master Canada once for all.

The plan was similar to the one which Amherst and Wolfe carried to success exactly fifty years

later, and with a Wolfe in command it might now
have succeeded. The troops from England were
to be at Boston before the end of May, 1709. The
colonial forces gathered. New Jersey and Pennsylvania refused, indeed, to send any soldiers; but
New York and the other colonies concerned did
their full share. By the early summer Colonel
Francis Nicholson, with some fifteen hundred
men, lay fully equipped in camp on Wood Creek
near Lake Champlain, ready to descend on Montreal as soon as news came of the arrival of the
British fleet at Boston for the attack on Quebec.
On the shores of Boston harbor lay another colonial army, large for the time — the levies from New
England which were to sail to Quebec. Officers
had come out from England to drill these hardy
men, and as soldiers they were giving a good account of themselves. They watched, fasted, and
prayed, and watched again for the fleet from England. Summer came and then autumn and still
the fleet did not arrive. Far away, in the crowded
camp on Wood Creek, pestilence broke out and as
time wore on this army slowly melted away either
by death or withdrawal. At last, on October 11,
1709, word came from the British ministry, dated
the 27th of July, two months after the promised

fleet was to arrive at Boston, that it had been sent instead to Portugal.

In spite of this disappointment the resolution endured to conquer Canada. New York joined New England in sending deputations to London to ask again for help. Four Mohawk chiefs went with Peter Schuyler from New York and were the wonder of the day in London. It is something to have a plan talked about. Malplaquet, the last of Marlborough's great victories, had been won in the autumn of 1709 and the thought of a new enterprise was popular. Nicholson, who had been sent from Boston, urged that the first step should be to take Port Royal. What the colonies required for this expedition was the aid of four frigates and five hundred soldiers who should reach Boston by March.

The help arrived, though not in March but in July, 1710. Boston was filled with enthusiasm for the enterprise. The legislature made military service compulsory, quartered soldiers in private houses without consent of the owners, impressed sailors, and altogether was quite arbitrary and high-handed. The people, however, would bear almost anything if only they could crush Port Royal, the den of privateers who seized many New

England vessels. On the 18th of September, to the great joy of Boston, the frigates and the transports sailed away, with Nicholson in command of the troops and Vetch as adjutant-general.

What we know today as Digby Basin on the east side of the Bay of Fundy, is a great harbor, landlocked but for a narrow entrance about a mile wide. Through this "gut," as it is called, the tide rushes in a torrential and dangerous stream, but soon loses its violence in the spacious and quiet harbor. Here the French had made their first enduring colony in America. On the shores of the beautiful basin the *fleurs-de-lis* had been raised over a French fort as early as 1605. A lovely valley opens from the head of the basin to the interior. It is now known as the Annapolis Valley, a fertile region dotted by the homesteads of a happy and contented people. These people, however, are not French in race nor do they live under a French Government. When on the 24th of September, 1710, the fleet from Boston entered the basin, and in doing so lost a ship and more than a score of men through the destructive current, the decisive moment had come for all that region. Fate had decreed that the land should not remain French but should become English.

Port Royal was at that time a typical French community of the New World. The village consisted of some poor houses made of logs or planks, a wooden church, and, lying apart, a fort defended by earthworks. The Governor, Subercase, was a brave French officer. He ruled the little community with a despotism tempered only by indignant protests to the King from those whom he ruled when his views and theirs did not coincide. The peasants in the village counted for nothing. Connected with the small garrison there were ladies and gentlemen who had no light opinion of their own importance and were so peppery that Subercase wished he had a madhouse in which to confine some of them. He thought well of the country. It produced, he said, everything that France produced except olives. The fertile land promised abundance of grain and there was an inexhaustible supply of timber. There were many excellent harbors. Had he a million *livres*, he would, he said, invest it gladly in the country and be certain of a good return. His enthusiasm had produced, however, no answering enthusiasm at Versailles, for there the interests of Port Royal were miserably neglected. Yet it was a thorn in the flesh of the English. In 1708 privateers from

Port Royal had destroyed no less than thirty-five English vessels, chiefly from Boston, and had carried to the fort four hundred and seventy prisoners. Even in winter months French ships would flit out of Port Royal and bring in richly laden prizes. Can we wonder at Boston's deep resolve that now at last the pest should end!

It was an imposing force which sailed into the basin. The four frigates and thirty transports carried an army far greater than Subercase had thought possible. The English landed some fourteen hundred men. Subercase had less than three hundred. Within a few days, when the English began to throw shells into the town, he asked for terms. On the 16th of October the little garrison, neglected by France and left ragged and half-starved, marched out with drums beating and colors flying. The English, drawn up before the gate, showed the usual honors to a brave foe. The French flag was hauled down and in its place floated that of Britain. Port Royal was renamed Annapolis and Vetch was made its Governor. Three times before had the English come to Port Royal as conquerors and then gone away, but now they were to remain. Ever since that October day, when autumn was coloring the abundant foliage of the lovely harbor, the British flag has waved over Annapolis. Because the flag waved there it was destined to wave over all Acadia, or Nova Scotia, and with Acadia in time went Canada.

A partial victory, however, such as the taking of Port Royal, was not enough for the aroused spirit of the English. They and their allies had beaten Louis XIV on the battlefields of Europe and had so worn out France that clouds and darkness were about the last days of the Grand Monarch now nearing his end. In America his agents were still drawing up papers outlining grandiose designs for mastering the continent and for proving that England's empire was near its fall, but Europe knew that France in the long war had been beaten. The right way to smite France in America was to rely upon England's naval power, to master the great highway of the St. Lawrence, to isolate Canada, and to strangle one by one the French settlements, beginning with Quebec.

There was malignant intrigue at the court of Queen Anne. One favorite, the Duchess of Marlborough, had just been disgraced, and another, Mrs. Masham, had been taken on by the weak and stupid Queen. The conquest of Canada, if it could be achieved without the aid of Marlborough, would

his much desired overthrow. Petty more unhappily at the root of the great
Who better to lead such an expedition
brother of the new favorite whose suc-
ht discredit the husband of the old one?
gly General "Jack" Hill, brother of
Masham, was appointed to the chief military
command and an admiral hitherto little known
but of good habits and quick wit, Sir Hovenden
Walker, was to lead the fleet.

The expedition against Quebec was on a scale
adequate for the time. Britain dispatched seven
regiments of regulars, numbering in all five
thousand five hundred men, and there were be-
sides in the fleet some thousands of sailors and
marines. Never before had the English sent to
North America a force so great. On June 24,
1711, Admiral Walker arrived at Boston with his
great array. Boston was impressed, but Boston
was also a little hurt, for the British leaders were
very lofty and superior in their tone towards colonials and gave orders as if Boston were a provincial city of England which must learn respect
and obedience to His Majesty's officers "vested
with the Queen's Royal Power and Authority."

More than seventy ships, led by nine men-of-

war, sailed from Boston for the attack on
On board were nearly twelve thousa
Compared with this imposing fleet, that of
twenty-one years earlier, seems feeble.
had set out too late.   This fleet was in good t
for it sailed on the 30th of July.   Vetch, alwa
competent, was in command of the colonial military forces, but never had any chance to show his
mettle, for during the voyage the seamen were in
control.   The Admiral had left England with secret
instructions.   He had not been informed of the
task before him and for it he was hardly prepared.
There were no competent pilots to correct his ig-
norance.   Now that he knew where he was going
he was anxious about the dangers of the northern
waters.   The St. Lawrence River, he believed,
froze solidly to the bottom in winter and he feared
that the ice would crush the sides of his ships.   As
he had provisions for only eight or nine weeks, his
men might starve.   His mind was filled, as he
himself says, with melancholy and dismal horror
at the prospect of seamen and soldiers, worn to
skeletons by hunger, drawing lots to decide who
should die first amidst the "adamantine frosts"
and "mountains of snow" of bleak and barren
Canada.

The Gulf and River St. Lawrence spell death to an incompetent sailor. The fogs, the numerous shoals and islands, make skillful seamanship necessary. It is a long journey from Boston to Quebec by water. For three weeks, however, all went well. On the 22d of August, Walker was out of sight of land in the Gulf where it is about seventy miles wide above the Island of Anticosti. A strong east wind with thick fog is dreaded in those waters even now, and on the evening of that day a storm of this kind blew up. In the fog Walker lost his bearings. When in fact he was near the north shore he thought he was not far from the south shore. At half-past ten at night Paddon, the captain of the *Edgar*, Walker's flagship, came to tell him that land was in sight. Walker assumed that it was the south shore and gave a fatal order for the fleet to turn and head northward, a change which turned them straight towards cliffs and breakers. He then went to bed. Soon one of the military officers rushed to his cabin and begged him to come on deck as the ships were among breakers. Walker, who was an irascible man, resented the intrusion and remained in bed. A second time the officer appeared and said the fleet would be lost if the Admiral did not act.

Why it was left for a military rather than a naval officer to rouse the Admiral in such a crisis we do not know. Perhaps the sailors were afraid of the great man. Walker appeared on deck in dressing gown and slippers. The fog had lifted, and in the moonlight there could be seen breaking surf to leeward. A French pilot, captured in the Gulf, had taken pains to give what he could of alarming information. He now declared that the ships were off the north shore. Walker turned his own ship sharply and succeeded in beating out into deep water and safety. For the fleet the night was terrible. Some ships dropped anchor which held, for happily the storm abated. Fog guns and lights as signals of distress availed little to the ships in difficulty. Eight British transports laden with troops and two ships carrying supplies were dashed to pieces on the rocks. The shrieks of drowning men could be heard in the darkness. The scene was the rocky Isle aux Œufs and adjacent reefs off the north shore. About seven hundred soldiers, including twenty-nine officers, and in addition perhaps two hundred sailors, were lost on that awful night.

The disaster was not overwhelming and Walker might have gone on and captured Quebec. He had not lost a single war-ship and he had still some eleven thousand men. General Hill might have stiffened the back of the forlorn Admiral, but Hill himself was no better. Vetch spoke for going on. He knew the St. Lawrence waters for he had been at Quebec and had actually charted a part of the river and was more familiar with it, he believed, than were the Canadians themselves. What pilots there were declared, however, that to go on was impossible and the helpless captains of the ships were of opinion that, with the warning of such a disaster, they could not disregard this counsel. Though the character of the English is such that usually a reverse serves to stiffen their backs, in this case it was not so. A council of war yielded to the panic of the hour and the great fleet turned homeward. Soon it was gathered in what is now Sydney harbor in Cape Breton. From here the New England ships went home and Walker sailed for England. At Spithead the *Edgar*, the flag-ship, blew up and all on board perished. Walker was on shore at the time. So far was he from being disgraced that he was given a new command. Later, when the Whigs came in, he was dismissed from the service, less, it seems, in blame for the disaster than for his Tory opinions.   It is not an unusual irony of life that Vetch, the one wholly efficient leader in the expedition, ended his days in a debtor's prison.

Quebec had shivered before a menace, the greatest in its history.   Through the long months of the summer of 1711 there had been prayer and fasting to avert the danger.   Apparently trading ships had deserted the lower St. Lawrence in alarm, for no word had arrived at Quebec of the approach of Walker's fleet.   Nor had the great disaster been witnessed by any onlookers.   The island where it occurred was then and still remains desert.   Up to the middle of October, nearly two months after the disaster, the watchers at Quebec feared that they might see any day a British fleet rounding the head of the Island of Orleans.   On the 19th of October the first news of the disaster arrived and then it was easy for Quebec to believe that God had struck the English wretches with a terrible vengeance.   Three thousand men, it was said, had reached land and then perished miserably. Many bodies had been found naked and in attitudes of despair.   Other thousands had perished in the water.   Vessel-loads of spoil had been gathered, rich plate, beautiful swords, magnificent clothing, gold, silver, jewels.   The truth seems to be that some weeks after the disaster the evidences of the wrecks were discovered. Even to this day ships are battered to pieces in those rock-strewn waters and no one survives to tell the story. Some fishermen landing on the island had found human bodies, dead horses and other animals, and the hulls of seven ships. They had gathered some wreckage — and that was the whole story. Quebec sang *Te Deum*. From attacks by sea there had now been two escapes which showed God's love for Canada. In the little church of *Notre Dame des Victoires*, consecrated at that time to the memory of the deliverance from Phips and Walker, daily prayers are still poured out for the well-being of Canada. God had been a present help on land as well as on the sea. Nicholson, with more than two thousand men, had been waiting at his camp near Lake Champlain to descend on Montreal as soon as Walker reached Quebec. When he received the news of the disaster he broke up his force and retired. For the moment Canada was safe from the threatened invasion.

In spite of this apparent deliverance, the long war, now near its end, brought a destructive blow to French power in America. Though France still possessed vigor and resources which her enemies were apt to underrate, the war had gone against her in Europe. Her finest armies had been destroyed by Marlborough, her taxation was crushing, her credit was ruined, her people were suffering for lack of food. The allies had begun to think that there was no humiliation which they might not put upon France. Louis XIV, they said, must give up Alsace, which, with Lorraine, he had taken some years earlier, and he must help to drive his own grandson from the Spanish throne. This exorbitant demand stirred the pride not only of Louis but of the French nation, and the allies found that they could not trample France under their feet. The Treaty of Utrecht, concluded in 1713, shows that each side was too strong as yet to be crushed. In dismissing Marlborough, Great Britain had lost one of her chief assets. His name had become a terror to France. To this day, both in France and in French Canada, is sung the popular ditty "Monsieur Malbrouck est mort," a song of delight at a report that Marlborough was dead. When in place of Marlborough leaders of the type of General Hill were appointed to high command, France could not be finally beaten. The Treaty of Utrecht was the outcome of war-weariness. It marks, however, a double check to

Louis XIV. He could not master Europe and he could not master America. France now ceded to Britain her claim to Acadia, Newfoundland, and Hudson Bay. She regarded this, however, as only a temporary set-back and was soon planning and plotting great designs far surpassing the narrower vision of the English colonies.

It was with a wry face, however, that France yielded Acadia. To retain it she offered to give up all rights in the Newfoundland fisheries, the nursery of her marine. Britain would not yield Acadia, dreading chiefly perhaps the wrath of New England which had conquered Port Royal. Britain, however, compromised on the question of boundaries in a way so dangerous that the long war settled finally no great issues in America. She took Acadia "according to its ancient limits," — but no one knew these limits. They were to be defined by a joint commission of the two nations which, after forty years, reached no agreement. The Island of Cape Breton and the adjoining Ile St. Jean, now Prince Edward Island, remained to France. Though Britain secured sovereignty over Newfoundland, France retained extensive rights in the Newfoundland fisheries. The treaty left unsettled the boundary between Canada and

5

the English colonies. While it yielded Hudson Bay to Britain, it settled nothing as to frontiers in the wilderness which stretched beyond the Great Lakes into the Far West and which had vast wealth in furs.

CHAPTER IV

LOUISBOURG AND BOSTON

For thirty years England and France now remained at peace, and England had many reasons for desiring peace to continue. Anne, the last of the Stuart rulers, died in 1714. The new King, George I, Elector of Hanover, was a German and a German unchangeable, for he was already fifty-four, with little knowledge of England and none of the English, and with an undying love for the dear despotic ways easily followed in a small German principality. He and his successor George II were thinking eternally of German rather than of English problems, and with German interests chiefly regarded it was well that England should make a friend of France. It was well, too, that under a new dynasty, with its title disputed, England should not encourage France to continue the friendly policy of Louis XIV towards James, the deposed Stuart Pretender. England had just made a new, determined, and arrogant enemy by forcing upon Spain the deep humiliation of ceding Gibraltar, which had been taken in 1704 by Admiral Rooke with allied forces. The proudest monarchy in Europe was compelled to see a spot of its own sacred territory held permanently by a rival nation. Gibraltar Spain was determined to recover. Its loss drove her into the arms of the enemies of England and remains to this day a grievance which on occasion Spanish politicians know well how to make useful.

Great Britain was now under the direction of a leader whose policy was peace. A nation is happy when a born statesman with a truly liberal mind and a genuine love of his country comes to the front in its affairs. Such a man was Sir Robert Walpole. He was a Whig squire, a plain country gentleman, with enough of culture to love good pictures and the ancient classics, but delighting chiefly in sports and agriculture, hard drinking and politics. When only twenty-seven he was already a leader among the Whigs; at thirty-two he was Secretary for War; and before he was forty he had become Prime Minister, a post which he really created and was the first Englishman to hold. Friendship with France marked a new phase of

British policy. Walpole's baffled enemies said that he was bribed by France. His shrewd insight kept France lukewarm in its support of the Stuart rising in 1715, which he punished with great severity. But it was as a master of finance that he was strongest. While continental nations were wasting men and money Walpole gloried in saving English lives and English gold. He found new and fruitful modes of taxation, but when urged to tax the colonies he preferred, as he said, to leave that to a bolder man. It is a pity that any one was ever found bold enough to do it.

Walpole's policy endured for a quarter of a century. He abandoned it only after a bitter struggle in which he was attacked as sacrificing the national honor for the sake of peace. Spain was an easy mark for those who wished to arouse the warlike spirit. She still persecuted and burned heretics, a great cause of offense in Protestant Britain, and she was rigorous in excluding foreigners from trading with her colonies. To be the one exception in this policy of exclusion was the privilege enjoyed by Britain. When the fortunes of Spain were low in 1713, she had been forced not merely to cede Gibraltar but also to give to the British the monopoly of supplying the Spanish colonies with negro slaves and the right to send one ship a year to trade at Porto Bello in South America. It seems a sufficiently ignoble bargain for a great nation to exact: the monopoly of carrying and selling cargoes of black men and the right to send a single ship yearly to a Spanish colony. We can hardly imagine grave diplomats of our day haggling over such terms. But the eighteenth century was not the twentieth. From the treaty the British expected amazing results. The South Sea Company was formed to carry on a vast trade with South America. One ship a year could, of course, carry little, but the ships laden with negroes could smuggle into the colonies merchandise and the one trading ship could be and was reloaded fraudulently from lighters so that its cargo was multiplied manyfold. Out of the belief in huge profits from this trade with its exaggerated visions of profit grew in 1720 the famous South Sea Bubble which inaugurated a period of frantic speculation in England. Worthless shares in companies formed for trade in the South Seas sold at a thousand per cent of their face value. It is a form of madness to which human greed is ever liable. Walpole's financial insight condemned from the first the wild outburst, and his common sense during the crisis helped to stem the tide of disaster. The South Sea Bubble burst partly because Spain stood sternly on her own rights and punished British smugglers. During many years the tension between the two nations grew. No doubt Spanish officials were harsh. Tales were repeated in England of their brutalities to British sailors who fell into their hands. In 1739 the story of a certain Captain Jenkins that his ear had been cut off by Spanish captors and thrown in his face with an insulting message to his government brought matters to a climax. Events in other parts of Europe soon made the war general. When, in 1740, the young King of Prussia, Frederick II, came to the throne, his first act was to march an army into Silesia. To this province he had, he said, in the male line, a better claim than that of the woman, Maria Theresa, who had just inherited the Austrian crown. Frederick conquered Silesia and held it. In 1744 he was allied with Spain and France, while Britain allied herself with Austria, and thus Britain and France were again at war.

In America both sides had long seen that the war was inevitable. Never had French opinion been more arrogant in asserting France's right to North America than after the Treaty of Utrecht.

At the dinner-table of the Governor in Quebec there was incessant talk of Britain's incapacity, of the sheer luck by which she had blundered into the occupation of great areas, while in truth she was weak through lack of union and organization. A natural antipathy, it was said, existed between her colonies and herself; she was a monarchy while they were really independent republics.   France, on the other hand, had grown stronger since the last war.   In 1713 she had retained the island of Cape Breton and now she had made it a new menace to British power.   Boston, which had breathed more freely after the fall of Port Royal in 1710, soon had renewed cause for alarm in regard to its shipping.   On the southern coast of Cape Breton, there was a spacious harbor with a narrow entrance easily fortified, and here France began to build the fortress of Louisbourg.   It was planned on the most approved military principles of the time.   Through its strength, the boastful talk went, France should master North America.   The King sent out cannon, undertook to build a hospital, to furnish chaplains for the service of the Church, to help education, and so on.   Above all, he sent to Louisbourg soldiers.

Reports of these wonderful things reached the

English colonies and caused fears and misgivings.
New England believed that Louisbourg reflected
the pomp and wealth of Versailles. The fortress
was, in truth, slow in building and never more
than a rather desolate outpost of France. It contained in all about four thousand people. During
the thirty years of the long truce it became so
strong that it was without a rival on the Atlantic coast. The excellent harbor was a haven for
the fishermen of adjacent waters and a base for
French privateers, who were a terror to all the near
trade routes of the Atlantic. On the military side
Louisbourg seemed a success. But the French
failed in their effort to colonize the island of Cape
Breton on which the fortress stood. Today this
island has great iron and other industries. There
are coal-mines near Louisbourg; and its harbor,
long deserted after the fall of the power of France,
has now an extensive commerce. The island was
indeed fabulously rich in coals and minerals. To
use these things, however, was to be the task of a
new age of industry. The colonist of the eighteenth century — a merchant, a farmer, or a fur
trader — thought that Cape Breton was bleak and
infertile and refused to settle there. Louisbourg
remained a compact fortress with a good harbor,

free from ice during most of the year, but too much haunted by fog. It looked out on a much-traveled sea. But it remained set in the wilderness.

Even if Louisbourg made up for the loss of Port Royal, this did not, however, console France for the cession of Acadia. The fixed idea of those who shaped the policy of Canada was to recover Acadia and meanwhile to keep its French settlers loyal to France. The Acadians were not a promising people with whom to work. In Acadia, or Nova Scotia, as the English called it, these backward people had slowly gathered during a hundred years and had remained remote and neglected. They had cleared farms, built primitive houses, planted orchards, and reared cattle. In 1713 their number did not exceed two or three thousand, but already they were showing the amazing fertility of the French race in America. They were prosperous but ignorant. Almost none of them could read. After the cession of their land to Britain in 1713 they had been guaranteed by treaty the free exercise of their religion and they were Catholics to a man. It seems as if history need hardly mention a people so feeble and obscure. Circumstances, however, made the rôle of the Acadians important. Their position was unique. The

Treaty of Utrecht gave them the right to leave Acadia within a year, taking with them their personal effects. To this Queen Anne added the just privilege of selling their lands and houses. Neither the Acadians themselves, however, nor their new British masters were desirous that they should leave. The Acadians were content in their old homes; and the British did not wish them to help in building up the neighboring French stronghold on Cape Breton. It thus happened that the French officials could induce few of the Acadians to migrate and the English troubled them little. Having been resolute in acquiring Nova Scotia, Britain proceeded straightway to neglect it. She brought in few settlers. She kept there less than two hundred soldiers and even to these she paid so little attention that sometimes they had no uniforms. The Acadians prospered, multiplied, and quarreled as to the boundaries of their lands. They rendered no military service, paid no taxes, and had the country to themselves as completely as if there had been no British conquest. They rarely saw a British official. If they asked the British Governor at Annapolis to settle for them some vexed question of rights or ownership he did so and they did not even pay a fee.

This is not, however, the whole story. England's neglect of the colony was France's opportunity. Perhaps the French court did not follow closely what was going on in Acadia. The successive French Governors of Canada at Quebec were, however, alert; and their policy was to incite the Abenaki Indians on the New England frontier to harass the English settlements, and to keep the Acadians an active factor in the support of French plans. The nature of French intrigue is best seen in the career of Sebastien Rale. He was a highly educated Jesuit priest. It was long a tradition among the Jesuits to send some of their best men as missionaries among the Indians. Rale spent nearly the whole of his life with the Abenakis at the mission station of Norridgewock on the Kennebec River. He knew the language and the customs of the Indians, attended their councils, and dominated them by his influence. He was a model missionary, earnest and scholarly. But the Jesuit of that age was prone to be half spiritual zealot, half political intriguer. There is no doubt that the Indians had a genuine fear that the English, with danger from France apparently removed by the Treaty of Utrecht, would press claims to lands about the Kennebec River in what is now the State of Maine, and that they would ignore the claims of the Indians and drive them out. The Governor at Quebec helped to arouse the savages against the arrogant intruders. English border ruffians stirred the Indians by their drunken outrages and gave them real cause for anger. The savages knew only one way of expressing political unrest. They began murdering women and children in raids on lonely log cabins on the frontier. The inevitable result was that in 1721 Massachusetts began a war on them which dragged on for years. Rale, inspired from Quebec, was believed to control the Indians and, indeed, boasted that he did so. At last the English struck at the heart of the trouble. In 1724 some two hundred determined men made a silent advance through the forest to the mission village of Norridgewock where Rale lived, and Rale died fighting the assailants. In Europe a French Jesuit such as he would have worked among diplomats and at the luxurious courts of kings. In America he worked among savages under the hard conditions of frontier life. The methods and the aims in both cases were the same — by subtle and secret influence so to mold the actions of men that France should be exalted in power. In their high politics the

French sometimes overreached themselves. To seize points of vantage, to intrigue for influence, are not in themselves creative. They must be supported by such practical efforts as will assure an economic reserve adequate in the hour of testing. France failed partly because she did not know how to lay sound industrial foundations which should give substance to the brilliant planning of her leaders.

To French influence of this kind the English opposed forces that were the outcome of their national character and institutions. They were keener traders than the French and had cheaper and better goods, with the exception perhaps of French gunpowder and of French brandy, which the Indians preferred to English rum. Though the English were less alert and less brilliant than the French, the work that they did was more enduring. Their settlements encroached ever more and more upon the forest. They found and tilled the good lands, traded and saved and gradually built up populous communities. The British colonies had twenty times the population of Canada. The tide of their power crept in slowly but it moved with the relentless force that has subsequently made nearly the whole of North America English in speech and modes of thought.

When, in 1744, open war between the two nations came at last in Europe, each prepared to spring at the other in America — and France sprang first. In Nova Scotia, on the narrow strait which separates the mainland from the island of Cape Breton, the British had a weak little fishing settlement called Canseau. Suddenly in May, 1744, when the British at Canseau had heard nothing of war, two armed vessels from Louisbourg with six or seven hundred soldiers and sailors appeared before the poor little place and demanded its surrender. To this the eighty British defenders agreed on the condition that they should be sent to Boston which, as yet, had not heard of the war. Meanwhile they were taken to Louisbourg where they kept their eyes open. But the French continued in their offensive. The one vital place held by the British in Nova Scotia was Annapolis, at that time so neglected that the sandy ramparts had crumbled into the ditch supposed to protect them, and cows from the neighboring fields walked up the slope and looked down into the fort. It was Duvivier, the captor of Canseau, who attacked Annapolis. He had hoped much for help from the

Indians and the Acadians, but, though both seemed
eager, both failed him in action.   Paul Mascarene,
who defended Annapolis, was of Huguenot blood,
which stimulated him to fight the better against
the Catholic French.   Boston sent him help, for
that little capital was deeply moved, and so
Annapolis did not fall, though it was harassed
during the whole summer of 1744; and New England, in a fever at the new perils of war, prepared
a mighty stroke against the French.

This expedition was to undertake nothing less
than the capture of Louisbourg itself.   The colonial troops had been so often reminded of their
inferiority to regular troops as fighting forces that,
with provincial docility, they had almost come to
accept the estimate.   It was well enough for them
to fight irregular French and Indian bands, but to
attack a fortress defended by a French garrison
was something that only a few bold spirits among
them could imagine.   Such a spirit, however, was
William Vaughan, a Maine trader, deeply involved
in the fishing industry and confronted with ruin
from hostile Louisbourg.   Shirley, the Governor
of Massachusetts, a man of eager ambition, took
up the proposal and worked out an elaborate plan.
The prisoners who had been captured at Canseau

by the French and interned at Louisbourg now arrived at Boston and told of bad conditions in the fortress. In January, 1745, Shirley called a session of the General Court, the little parliament of Massachusetts, and, having taken the unusual step of pledging the members to secrecy, he unfolded his plan. But it proved too bold for the prudent legislators, and they voted it down. Meanwhile New England trade was suffering from ships which used Louisbourg as a base. At length public opinion was aroused and, when Shirley again called the General Court, a bare majority endorsed his plan. Soon thereafter New England was aflame. Appeals for help were sent to England and, it is said, even to Jamaica. Shirley counted on aid from a British squadron, under Commodore Peter Warren, in American waters, but at first Warren had no instructions to help such a plan. This disappointment did not keep New England from going on alone. In the end Warren received instructions to give the necessary substantial aid, and he established a strict blockade which played a vital part in the siege of the French fortress.

In this hour of deadly peril Louisbourg was in not quite happy case. Some of the French

6

officers, who would otherwise have starved on their low pay, were taking part in illicit trade and were neglecting their duties. Just after Christmas in 1744, there had been a mutiny over a petty question of butter and bacon. Here, as in all French colonies, there were cliques, with the suspicions and bitterness which they involve. The Governor Duchambon, though brave enough, was a man of poor judgment in a position that required both tact and talent. The English did not make the mistake of delaying their preparations. They were indeed so prompt that they arrived at Canseau early in April and had to wait for the ice to break up in Gabarus Bay, near Louisbourg, where they intended to land. Here, on April 30, the great fleet appeared. A watcher in Louisbourg counted ninety-six ships standing off shore. With little opposition from the French the amazing army landed at Freshwater Cove.

Then began an astonishing siege. The commander of the New England forces, William Pepperrell, was a Maine trader, who dealt in a little of everything, fish, groceries, lumber, ships, land. Though innocent of military science, he was firm and tactful. A British officer with strict military ideas could not, perhaps, have led that strange

army with success. Pepperrell knew that he had
good fighting material; he knew, too, how to handle
it. In his army of some four thousand men there
was probably not one officer with a regular training.
Few of his force had proper equipment, but nearly
all his men were handy on a ship as well as on land.
In Louisbourg were about two thousand defenders,
of whom only five or six hundred were French
regulars. These professional soldiers watched with
contempt not untouched with apprehension the
breaches of military precedent in the operations of
the besiegers. Men harnessed like horses dragged
guns through morasses into position, exposed themselves recklessly, and showed the skill, initia-
tive, and resolution which we have now come to
consider the dominant qualities of the Yankee.
In time Warren arrived with a British squadron
and then the French were puzzled anew. They
could not understand the relations between the
fleet and the army, which seemed to them to
belong to different nations. The New Englanders
appeared to be under a Governor who was something like an independent monarch. He had
drawn up elaborate plans for his army, comical
in their apparent disregard of the realities of war,
naming the hour when the force should land "un-

observed" before Louisbourg, instructing Pepperrell to surprise that place while every one was
asleep, and so on. Kindly Providence was expected even to give continuous good weather. "The
English appear to have enlisted Heaven in their interests," said a despairing resident of the town;
"so long as the expedition lasted they had the
most beautiful weather in the world."   There
were no storms; the winds were favorable; fog, so
common on that coast, did not creep in; and the
sky was clear.

Among the French the opinion prevailed that
the English colonists were ferocious pirates plotting
eternally to destroy the power of France. Their
liberty, however, it was well understood, had made
them strong; and now they quickly became formidable soldiers. Their shooting, bad at first, was,
in the end, superb. Sometimes in their excess of
zeal they overcharged their cannon so that the guns
burst.   But they managed to hit practically every
house in Louisbourg, and since most of the houses
were of wood there was constant danger of fire.
Some of the French fought well. Even children
of ten and twelve helped to carry ammunition.

The Governor Duchambon tried to keep up the
spirits of the garrison by absurd exaggeration of

British losses.   He was relying much on help from France, but only a single ship reached port.   On May 19, 1745, the besieged saw approaching Louisbourg a great French ship of war, the *Vigilant*, long looked for, carrying 64 guns and 560 men. A northwest wind was blowing which would have brought her quickly into the harbor.   The British fleet was two and a half leagues away to leeward. The great ship, thinking herself secure, did not even stop to communicate with Louisbourg but wantonly gave chase to a small British privateer which she encountered near the shore.   By skillful maneuvering the smaller ship led the French frigate out to sea again, and then the British squadron came up.   From five o'clock to ten in the evening anxious men in Louisbourg watched the fight and saw at last the *Vigilant* surrender after losing eighty men.   This disaster broke the spirit of the defenders, who were already short of ammunition. When they knew that the British were preparing for a combined assault by land and sea, they made terms and surrendered on the 17th of June, after the siege had lasted for seven weeks.   The garrison marched out with the honors of war, to be transported to France, together with such of the civilian population as wished to go.

The British squadron then sailed into the harbor. Pepperrell's strange army, ragged and war-worn after the long siege, entered the town by the south gate. They had fought as crusaders, for to many of them Catholic Louisbourg was a stronghold of Satan. Whitfield, the great English evangelist, then in New England, had given them a motto — *Nil desperandum Christo duce.* There is a story that one of the English chaplains, old Parson Moody, a man of about seventy, had brought with him from Boston an axe and was soon found using it to hew down the altar and images in the church at Louisbourg. If the story is true, it does something to explain the belief of the French in the savagery of their opponents who would so treat things which their enemies held to be most sacred. The French had met this fanaticism with a savagery equally intense and directed not against things but against the flesh of men. An inhabitant of Louisbourg during the siege describes the dauntless bravery of the Indian allies of the French during the siege: "Full of hatred for the English whose ferocity they abhor, they destroy all upon whom they can lay hands." He does not have even a word of censure for the savages who tortured and killed in cold blood a party of some twenty English who had been induced to surrender on promise of life. The French declared that not they but the savages were responsible for such barbarities, and the English retorted that the French must control their allies. Feeling on such things was naturally bitter on both sides and did much to decide that the war between the two nations should be to the death.

The fall of Louisbourg brought great exultation to the English colonies. It was a unique event, the first prolonged and successful siege that had as yet taken place north of Mexico. An odd chance of war had decreed that untrained soldiers should win a success so prodigious. New England, it is true, had incurred a heavy expenditure, and her men, having done so much, naturally imagined that they had done everything, and talked as if the siege was wholly their triumph. They were, of course, greatly aided by the fleet under Warren, and the achievement was a joint triumph of army and navy. New England alone, however, had the credit of conceiving and of arousing others to carry out a brilliant exploit.

Victory inspires to further victory. The British, exultant after Louisbourg, were resolved to make an end of French power in America. *"Delenda est Canada!"* cried Governor Shirley to the General Court of Massachusetts, and the response of the members was the voting of men and money on a scale that involved the bankruptcy of the Commonwealth. Other colonies, too, were eager for a cause which had won a success so dazzling, and some eight thousand men were promised for an attack on Canada, proud and valiant Massachusetts contributing nearly one-half of the total number. The old plan was to be followed. New York was to lead in an attack by way of Lake Champlain. New England was to collect its forces at Louisbourg. Here a British fleet should come, carrying eight battalions of British regulars, and, with Warren in command, the whole armada should proceed to Quebec. Nothing came of this elaborate scheme. Neither the promised troops nor the fleet arrived from England. British ministers broke faith with the colonists in the adventure with quite too light a heart.

Stories went abroad of disorder and dissension in Louisbourg under the English and of the weakness of the place. Disease broke out. Hundreds of New England soldiers died and their bones now lie in graves, unmarked and forgotten, on the seashore by the deserted fortress; at almost any time still their bones, washed down by the waves, may be picked up on the beach. There were sullen mutterings of discontent at Louisbourg. Soldiers grumbled over grievances which were sometimes fantastic. Rumor had been persistent in creating a legend that vast wealth, the accumulated plunder brought in by French privateers, was stored in the town. From this source a rich reward in booty was expected by the soldiers. In fact, when Louisbourg was taken, all looting was forbidden and the soldiers were put on guard over houses which they had hoped to rob. For the soldiers there were no prizes. Louisbourg was poor. The sailors, on the other hand, were fortunate. As a decoy Warren kept the French flag flying over the harbor, and French ships sailed in, one of them with a vast treasure of gold and silver coin and ingots from Peru valued at £600,000. One other prize was valued at £200,000 and a third at £140,000. Warren's own share of prize money amounted to £60,000, while Pepperrell, the unrewarded leader of the sister service, piled up a personal debt of £10,000. Quarrels occurred between soldiers and sailors, and in these the New Englanders soon proved by no means the cowards which

complacent superiority in England considered
them; rather, as an enlightened Briton said, "If
they had pickaxe and spade they would dig a way
to Hell itself and storm that stronghold."

Behind all difficulties was the question whether,
having taken Louisbourg, the British could continue to hold it.   France answered with a resolute
"No."   To retake it she fitted out a great fleet.
Nearly half her navy gathered under the Duc
d'Anville and put to sea on June 20, 1746.   If in
the previous summer God had helped the English
with good weather, by a similar proof His face
now appeared turned a second time against the
French.   In the great array there were more than
sixty ships, which were to gather at Chebucto,
now Halifax, harbor, and to be joined there by four
great ships of war from the West Indies.   Everything went wrong.   On the voyage across the
Atlantic there was a prolonged calm, followed by a
heavy squall.   Several ships were struck by light-
ning.   A magazine on the *Mars* blew up, killing
ten and wounding twenty-one men.   Pestilence
broke out.   As a crowning misfortune, the fleet
was scattered by a terrific storm.   After great
delay d'Anville's ship reached Chebucto, then a
wild and lonely spot.   The expected fleet from the

Vest Indies had indeed come, but had gone, since
he ships from France, long overdue, had not
rrived. D'Anville died suddenly — some said of
apoplexy, others of poison self-administered. More
ships arrived full of sick men and short of provisions. D'Estournel, who succeeded d'Anville in
chief command, in despair at the outlook killed
himself with his own sword after the experience of
only a day or two in his post. La Jonquière, a competent officer, afterwards Governor of Canada, then
led the expedition. The pestilence still raged, and
from two to three thousand men died. One day a
Boston sloop boldly entered Chebucto harbor to
find out what was going on. It is a wonder that the
British did not descend upon the stricken French
and destroy them. In October, La Jonquière, having pulled his force together, planned to win the
small success of taking Annapolis, but again storms
scattered his ships. At the end of October he
finally decided to return to France. But there
were more heavy storms; and one French crew
was so near starvation that only a chance meeting with a Portuguese ship kept them from killing
and eating five English prisoners. Only a battered remnant of the fleet eventually reached home
ports.

The disaster did not crush France. In May of the next spring, 1747, a new fleet under La Jonquière set out to retake Louisbourg. Near the coast of Europe, however, Admirals Anson and Warren met and completely destroyed it, taking prisoner La Jonquière himself. This disaster effected what was really the most important result of the war: it made the British fleet definitely superior to the French. During the struggle England had produced a new Drake, who attacked Spain in the spirit of the sea-dogs of Elizabeth. Anson had gone in 1740 into the Pacific, where he seized and plundered Spanish ships as Drake had done nearly two centuries earlier; and in 1744, when he had been given up for lost, he completed the great exploit of sailing round the world and bringing home rich booty. Such feats went far to give Britain that command of the sea on which her colonial Empire was to depend.

The issue of the war hung more on events that occurred in Europe than in America, and France had made gains as well as suffered losses. It was on the sea that she had sustained her chief defeats. In India she had gained by taking the English factory at Madras; and in the Low Countries she was still aggressive. Indeed, during the war England had been more hostile to Spain than to France. She had not taken very seriously her support of the colonies in their attack on Louisbourg and she had failed them utterly in their designs on Canada. It is true that in Europe England had grave problems to solve. Austria, with which she was allied, desired her to fight until Frederick of Prussia should give up the province of Silesia seized by him in 1740. In this quarrel England had no vital interest. France had occupied the Austrian Netherlands and had refused to hand back to Austria this territory unless she received Cape Breton in return. Britain might have kept Cape Breton if she would have allowed France to keep Belgium. This, in loyalty to Austria, she would not do. Accordingly peace was made at Aix-la-Chapelle in 1748 on the agreement that each side should restore to the other its conquests, not merely in Europe but also in America and Asia. Thus it happened that the British flag went up again at Madras while it came down at Louisbourg.

Boston was of course angry at the terms of the treaty. What sacrifices had Massachusetts not made! The least of them was the great burden of debt which she had piled up. Her sons had borne what Pepperrell called "almost incredible hardships." They had landed cannon on a lee shore when the great waves pounded to pieces their boats and when men wading breast high were crushed by the weight of iron. Harnessed two and three hundred to a gun, they had dragged the pieces one after the other over rocks and through bog and slime, and had then served them in the open under the fire of the enemy. New Englanders had died like "rotten sheep" in Louisbourg. The graves of nearly a thousand of them lay on the bleak point outside the wall. What they had gained by this sacrifice must now be abandoned. A spirit of discontent with the mother country went abroad and, after this sacrifice of colonial interests, never wholly died out. It is not without interest to note in passing that Gridley, the engineer who drew the plan of the defenses of Louisbourg, thirty years later drew those of Bunker Hill to protect men of the English race who fought against England.

Every one knew that the peace of 1748 was only a truce and Britain began promptly new defenses. Into the spacious harbor of Chebucto, which three years earlier had been the scene of the sorrows of d'Anville's fleet, there sailed in June, 1749, a considerable British squadron bent on a momentous errand. It carried some thousands of settlers, Edward Cornwallis, a governor clothed with adequate authority, and a force sufficient for the defense of the new foundation. Cornwallis was delighted with the prospect. "All the officers agree the harbour is the finest they have ever seen" — this, of Halifax harbor with the great Bedford Basin, opening beyond it, spacious enough to contain the fleets of the world. "The Country is one continuous Wood, no clear spot to be seen or heard of. D'Anville's fleet . . . cleared no ground; they encamped their men on the beach." The garrison was withdrawn from Louisbourg and soon arrived at Halifax, with a vast quantity of stores. A town was marked out; lots were drawn for sites; and every one knew where he might build his house. There were prodigious digging, chopping, hammering. "I shall be able to get them all Houses before winter," wrote Cornwallis cheerily. Firm military discipline, indeed, did wonders. Before winter came, a town had been created, and with the town a fortress which from that time has remained the chief naval and military stronghold of Great Britain in North America. At Louisbourg some two hundred miles farther east on the coast,

France could reëstablish her military strength, but now Louisbourg had a rival and each was resolved to yield nothing to the other. The founding of Halifax was in truth the symbol of the renewal of the struggle for a continent.

CHAPTER V

THE GREAT WEST

In days before the railway had made possible a
bulky commerce by overland routes, rivers furnished the chief means of access to inland regions.
The fame of the Ganges, the Euphrates, the Nile,
and the Danube shows the part which great rivers
have played in history. Of North America's four
greatest river systems, the two in the far north
have become known in times so recent that their
place in history is not yet determined. One of
them, the Mackenzie, a mighty stream some two
thousand miles long, flows into the Arctic Ocean
through what remains chiefly a wilderness. The
waters of the other, the Saskatchewan, discharge
into Hudson Bay more than a thousand miles
from their source, flowing through rich prairie
land which is still but scantily peopled. On the
Saskatchewan, as on the remaining two systems,
the St. Lawrence and the Mississippi, the French

7   97

were the pioneers. Though today the regions drained by these four rivers are dominated by the rival race, the story which we now follow is one of romantic enterprise in which the honors are with France.

More perhaps by accident than by design had the French been the first to settle on the St. Lawrence. Fishing vessels had hovered round the entrance to the Gulf of St. Lawrence for years before, in 1535, the French sailor, Jacques Cartier, advanced up the river as far as the foot of the torrential rapids where now stands the city of Montreal. Cartier was seeking a route to the Far East. He half believed that this impressive waterway drained the plains of China and that around the next bend he might find the busy life of an oriental city. The time came when it was known that a great sea lay between America and Asia and the mystery of the pathway to this sea long fascinated the pioneers of the St. Lawrence. Canada was a colony, a trading-post, a mission, the favorite field of Jesuit activity, but it was also the land which offered by way of the St. Lawrence a route leading illimitably westward to the Far East.

One other route rivaled the St. Lawrence in

promise, and that was the Mississippi. The two
rivers are essentially different in their approaches
and in type. The mouth of the St. Lawrence
opens directly towards Europe and of all American
rivers lies nearest to the seafaring peoples of
Europe. Since it flows chiefly in a rocky bed, its
course changes little; its waters are clear, and they
become icy cold as they approach the sea and
mingle with the tide which flows into the great
Gulf of St. Lawrence from the Arctic regions.
The Mississippi, on the other hand, is a turbid,
warm stream, flowing through soft lands. Its
shifting channel is divided at its mouth by deltas
created from the vast quantity of soil which the
river carries in its current. On the low-lying,
forest-clad, northern shore of the Gulf of Mexico
it was not easy to find the mouth of the Mississippi
by approaching it from the sea. The voyage there
from France was long and difficult; and, moreover, Spain claimed the lands bordering on the
Gulf of Mexico and declared herself ready to drive
out all intruders.

Nature, it is clear, dictated that, if France was
to build up her power in the interior of the New
World, it was the valley of the St. Lawrence which
she should first occupy. Time has shown the

riches of the lands drained by the St. Lawrence. On no other river system in the world is there now such a multitude of great cities. The modern traveler who advances by this route to the sources of the river beyond the Great Lakes surveys wonders ever more impressive. Before his view appear in succession Quebec, Montreal, Toronto, Buffalo, Cleveland, Detroit, Chicago, Duluth, and many other cities and towns, with millions in population and an aggregate of wealth so vast as to stagger the imagination. Step by step had the French advanced from Quebec to the interior. Champlain was on Lake Huron in 1615, and there the Jesuits soon had a flourishing mission to the Huron Indians. They had only to follow the shore of Lake Huron to come to the St. Mary's River bearing towards the sea the chilly waters of Lake Superior. On this river, a much frequented fishing ground of the natives, they founded the mission of Sainte Marie du Saut. Farther to the south, on the narrow opening connecting Lake Huron and Lake Michigan, grew up the post known as Michilimackinac. It was then inevitable that explorers and missionaries should press on into both Lake Superior and Lake Michigan. By the time that Frontenac came first to Canada in 1672 the French had a post called St. Esprit on the south shore of Lake Superior near its western end and they had also passed westward from Lake Michigan and founded posts on both the Illinois and the Wisconsin Rivers which flow into the Mississippi.

France had placed on record her claim to the whole of the Great West. On a June morning in 1671 there had been a striking scene at Sainte Marie du Saut. The French had summoned a great throng of Indians to the spot. There, with impressive ceremony, Saint-Lusson, an officer from Canada, had set up a cedar post on which was a plate engraved with the royal arms, and proclaimed Louis XIV lord of all the Indian tribes and of all the lands, rivers, and lakes, discovered and to be discovered in the region stretching from the Atlantic to that other mysterious sea beyond the spreading lands of the West. Henceforth at their peril would the natives disobey the French King, or other states encroach upon these his lands. A Jesuit priest followed Saint-Lusson with a description to the savages of their new lord, the King of France. He was master of all the other rulers of the world. At his word the earth trembled. He could set earth and sea on fire by the blaze of his cannon. The priest knew the temper of his savage audience and told of the King's warriors covered with the blood of his enemies, of the rivers of blood which flowed from their wounds, of the King's countless prisoners, of his riches and his power, so great that all the world obeyed him. The savages gave delighted shouts at the strange ceremony, but of its real meaning they knew nothing. What they understood was that the French seemed to be good friends who brought them muskets, hatchets, cloth, and especially the loved but destructive firewater which the savage palate ever craved.

The mystery of the Great Lakes once solved, there still remained that of the Western Sea. The St. Lawrence flowed eastward. Another river must therefore be found flowing westward. The French were eager listeners when the savages talked of a mighty river in the west flowing to the sea. They meant, as we now suppose, the Mississippi. There are vague stories of Frenchmen on the Mississippi at an earlier date; but, however this may be, it is certain that in the summer of 1673 Louis Joliet, the son of a wagon-maker of Quebec, and Jacques Marquette, a Jesuit priest, reached and descended the great river from the mouth of the Wisconsin to a point far past the mouth of the Ohio.

France thus planted herself on the Mississippi, though there her occupation was less complete and thorough than it was on the St. Lawrence. Distance was an obstacle; it was a far cry from Quebec by land, and from France the voyage by sea through the Gulf of Mexico was hardly less difficult. The explorer La Salle tried both routes. In 1681–1682 he set out from Montreal, reached the Mississippi overland, and descended to its mouth. Two years later he sailed from France with four ships bound for the mouth of the river, there to establish a colony; but before achieving his aim he was murdered in a treacherous attack led by his own countrymen.

It was Pierre Le Moyne, Sieur d'Iberville, who first made good France's claim to the Mississippi. He reached the river by sea in 1699 and ascended to a point some eighty miles beyond the present city of New Orleans. Farther east, on Biloxi Bay, he built Fort Maurepas and planted his first colony. Spain disliked this intrusion; but Spain — soon to be herself ruled, as France then was, by a Bourbon king — did not prove irreconcilable and slowly France built up a colony in the south. It was in 1718 that Iberville's brother, Jean Baptiste Le Moyne, Sieur de Bienville, founded New Orleans, destined to become in time one of the great cities of North America. Its beginnings were not propitious. The historian Charlevoix describes it as being in 1721 a low-lying, malarious place, infested by snakes and alligators, and consisting of a hundred wretched hovels.

In spite of this dreary outlook, it was still true that France, planted at the mouth of the Mississippi, controlled the greatest waterway in the world. Soon she had scattered settlements stretching northward to the Ohio and the Missouri, the one river reaching eastward almost to the waters of the St. Lawrence system, the other flowing out of the western plains from its source in the Rocky Mountains. The old mystery, however, remained, for the Mississippi flowed into the Gulf of Mexico, into Atlantic waters already well known. The route to the Western Sea was still to be found.

It was easy enough for France to record a sweeping claim to the West, but to make good this claim she needed a chain of posts, which should also be forts, linking the Mississippi with the St. Lawrence and strong enough to impress the Indians

whose country she had invaded. At first she had
reached the interior by way of the Ottawa River
and Lake Huron, and in that northern country
her position was secure enough through her posts
on the upper lakes. The route farther south by
Lake Ontario and Lake Erie was more difficult.
The Iroquois menaced Niagara and long refused
to let France have a footing there to protect her
pathway to Lake Erie and the Ohio Valley. It
was not until 1720, a period comparatively late,
that the French managed to have a fort at the
mouth of the Niagara. On the Detroit River, the
next strategic point on the way westward, they
were established earlier. Just after Frontenac
died in 1698, La Mothe Cadillac urged that there
should be built on this river a fort and town which
might be made the center of all the trading interests west of Lake Erie. End the folly, he urged,
of going still farther afield among the Indians
and teaching them the French language and
French modes of thought. Leave the Indians to
live their own type of life, to hunt and to fish.
They need European trade and they have valuable furs to exchange. Encourage them to come
to the French at Detroit and see that they go no-
where else by not allowing any other posts in the

western country. Cadillac was himself a keen if
secret participant in the profits of the fur trade
and hoped to be placed in command at Detroit
and there to become independent of control
from Quebec. Detroit was founded in 1701; and
though for a long time it did not thrive, the fact
that on the site has grown up one of the great industrial cities of modern times shows that Cadillac
had read aright the meaning of the geography of
North America.

When France was secure at Niagara and at
Detroit, two problems still remained unsolved.
One was that of occupying the valley of the Ohio,
the waters of which flow westward almost from
the south shore of Lake Erie until they empty
into the vaster flood of the Mississippi. Here
there was a lion in the path, for the English claimed
this region as naturally the hinterland of the colonies of Virginia and Pennsylvania. What happened
on the Ohio we shall see in a later chapter. The
other great problem, to be followed here, was to
explore the regions which lay beyond the Mississippi. These spread into a remote unknown, un-
explored by the white man, and might ultimately
lead to the Western Sea. We might have supposed that France's farther adventure into the

West would have been from the Mississippi up its great tributary the Missouri, which flows eastward from the eternal snows of the Rocky Mountains. Always, however, the uncertain temper of the many Indian tribes in this region made the advance difficult. The tribes inhabiting the west bank of the Mississippi were especially restless and savage. The Sioux, in particular, made life perilous for the French at their posts near the mouth of the Missouri.

It thus happened that the white man first reached the remoter West by way of regions farther north. It became easy enough to coast along the north and the south shore of Lake Superior, easy enough to find rivers which fed the great system of the St. Lawrence or of the Mississippi. These, however, would not solve the mystery. A river flowing westward was still to be sought. Thus, both in pursuit of the fur trade and in quest of the Western Sea, the French advanced westward from Lake Superior. Where now stands the city of Fort William there flows into Lake Superior the little stream called still by its Indian name of Kaministiquia. There the French had long maintained a trading-post from which they made adventurous journeys northward and westward.

The rugged regions still farther north had already been explored, at least in outline. There lay the great inland sea known as Hudson Bay. French and English had long disputed for its mastery. By 1670 the English had found trade to Hudson Bay so promising that they then created the Hudson's Bay Company, which remains one of the great trading corporations of the world. With the English on Hudson Bay, New France was between English on the north and English on the south and did not like it. On Hudson Bay the English showed the same characteristics which they had shown in New England. They were not stirred by vivid imaginings of what might be found westward beyond the low-lying coast of the great inland sea. They came for trade, planted themselves at the mouths of the chief rivers, unpacked their goods, and waited for the natives to come to barter with them. For many years the natives came, since they must have the knives, hatchets, and firearms of Europe. To share this profitable trade the French, now going overland to the north from Quebec, now sailing into Hudson Bay by the Straits, attacked the English; and on those dreary waters, long before the Great West was known, there had been many a naval battle, many a hand-to-hand fight for forts and their rich prize of furs.

The chief French hero in this struggle was that son of Charles Le Moyne of Montreal, Pierre Le Moyne d'Iberville, who ended his days in the task of founding the French colony of Louisiana. He was perhaps the most notable of all the adventurous leaders whom New France produced. He was first on Hudson Bay in the late summer of 1686, in a party of about a hundred men, led by the Chevalier de Troyes, who had marched overland from Quebec through the wilderness. The English on the Bay, with a charter from King Charles II, the friend of the French, and in a time of profound peace under his successor, thought themselves secure. They now had, however, a rude awakening. In the dead of night the Frenchmen fell upon Fort Hayes, captured its dazed garrison, and looted the place. The same fate befell all the other English posts on the Bay. Iberville gained a rich store of furs as his share of the plunder and returned with it to Quebec in 1687, just at the time when La Salle, that other pioneer of France, was struck down in the distant south by a murderer's hand.

Iberville was, above all else, a sailor. The

easiest route to Hudson Bay was by way of the sea. More than once after his first experience he led to the Bay a naval expedition. His exploits are still remembered with pride in French naval annals. In 1697 he sailed the *Pelican* through the ice-floes of Hudson Straits. He was attacked by three English merchantmen, with one hundred and twenty guns against his forty-four. One of the English ships escaped, one Iberville sank with all on board, one he captured. That autumn the hardy corsair was in France with a great booty from the furs which the English had laboriously gathered.

The triumph of the French on Hudson Bay was short-lived. Their exploits, though brilliant and daring, were more of the nature of raids than attempts to settle and explore. They did no more than the English to ascend the Nelson or other rivers to find what lay beyond; and in 1713, by the Treaty of Utrecht, as we have already seen, they gave up all claim to Hudson Bay and yielded that region to the English.

Pierre Gaultier de Varennes, Sieur de la Vérendrye, was a member of the Canadian *noblesse*, a son of the Governor of Three Rivers on the St.

seeming, however, he became just a fur trader and a successful one. We find him, in 1726, at the trading-post of Nipigon, not far from the lake of that name, near the north shore of Lake Superior. From this point it was not very difficult to reach the shore of one great sea, Hudson Bay, but that was not the Western Sea which fired his imagination. Incessantly he questioned the savages with whom he traded about what lay in the unknown West. His zeal was kindled anew by the talk of an Indian named Ochagach. This man said that he himself had been on a great lake lying west of Lake Superior, that out of it flowed a river westward, that he had paddled down this river until he came to water which, as La Vérendrye understood, rose and fell like the tide. Farther, to the actual mouth of the river, the savage had not gone, for fear of enemies, but he had been told that it emptied into a great body of salt water upon the shores of which lived many people. We may be sure that La Vérendrye read into the words of the savage the meaning which he himself desired and that in reality the Indian was describing only the waters which flow into Lake Winnipeg.

La Vérendrye was all eagerness. Soon we find

8

him back at Quebec stirring by his own enthusiasm the zeal of the Marquis de Beauharnois, the Governor of Canada, and begging for help to pay and equip a hundred men for the great enterprise in the West. The Governor did what he could but was unable to move the French court to give money. The sole help offered was a monopoly of the fur trade in the region to be explored, a doubtful gift, since it angered all the traders excluded from the monopoly. La Vérendrye, however, was able, by promising to hand over most of the profits, to persuade merchants in Montreal to equip him with the necessary men and merchandise.

There followed a period of high hopes and of heart-breaking failure. In 1731 La Vérendrye set out for the West with three sons, a nephew, a Jesuit priest, the Indian Ochagach as guide — a party numbering in all about fifty. He intended to build trading-posts as he went westward and to make the last post always a base from which to advance still farther. His difficulties read like those of Columbus. His men not only disliked the hard work which was inevitable but were haunted by superstitious fears of malignant fiends in the unknown land who were ready to punish the invaders of their secrets. The route lay across the rough country beyond Lake Superior. There were many long portages over which his men must carry the provisions and heavy stores for trade. At length the party reached Rainy Lake, and out of Rainy Lake the waters flow westward. The country seemed delightful. Fish and game were abundant, and it was not hard to secure a rich store of furs. On the shore of the lake, in a charming meadow surrounded by oak trees, La Vérendrye built a trading-post on waters flowing to the west, naming it Fort St. Pierre.

The voyageurs could now travel westward with the current. It is certain that other Frenchmen had preceded them in that region, but this is the first voyage of discovery of which we have any details. Escorted by an imposing array of fifty canoes of Indians, La Vérendrye floated down Rainy River to the Lake of the Woods, and here, on a beautiful peninsula jutting out into the lake, he built another post, Fort St. Charles. It must have seemed imposing to the natives. On walls one hundred feet square were four bastions and a watchtower; evidence of the perennial need of alertness and strength in the Indian country. There were a chapel, houses for the commandant and the priest, a powder-magazine, a storehouse, and other buildings. La Vérendrye cleared some land and planted wheat, and was thus the pioneer in the mighty wheat production of the West. Fish and game were abundant and the outlook was smiling. By this time the second winter of La Vérendrye's adventurous journeying was near, but even the cold of that hard region could not chill his eagerness. He himself waited at Fort St. Charles but his eldest son, Jean Baptiste, set out to explore still farther.

We may follow with interest the little group of Frenchmen and Indian guides as they file on snowshoes along the surface of the frozen river or over the deep snow of the silent forest on, ever on, to the West. They are the first white men of whom we have certain knowledge to press beyond the Lake of the Woods into that great Northwest so full of meaning for the future. The going was laborious and the distances seemed long, for on their return they reported that they had gone a hundred and fifty leagues, though in truth the distance was only a hundred and fifty miles. Then at last they stood on the shores of a vast body of water, ice-bound and forbidding as it lay in the grip of winter. It opened out illimitably westward. But it was not the Western Sea, for its waters were fresh. The shallow waters of Lake Winnipeg empty not into the Western Sea but into the Atlantic by way of Hudson Bay. Its shores then were deserted and desolate, and even to this day they are but scantily peopled. In that wild land there was no hint of the populous East of which La Vérendrye had dreamed.

At the mouth of the Winnipeg River, where it enters Lake Winnipeg, La Vérendrye built Fort Maurepas, named after the French minister who was in charge of the colonies and who was influential at court. The name no doubt expresses some clinging hope which La Vérendrye still cherished of obtaining help from the King. Already he was hard pressed for resources. Where were the means to come from for this costly work of building forts? From time to time he sent eastward canoes laden with furs which, after a long and difficult journey, reached Montreal. The traders to whom the furs were consigned sold them and kept the money as their own on account of their outlay. La Vérendrye in the far interior could not pay his men and would soon be without goods to trade with the Indians. After having repeatedly begged for help but in vain, he made a rapid journey to Montreal and implored the Governor to aid an enterprise which might change the outlook of the whole world. The Governor was willing but without the consent of France could not give help. By promising the traders, who were now partners in his monopoly, profits of one hundred per cent on their outlay, La Vérendrye at last secured what he needed. His canoes were laden with goods, and soon brawny arms were driving once again the graceful craft westward. He had offered a new hostage to fortune by arranging that his fourth son, a lad of eighteen, should follow him in the next year.

La Vérendrye pressed on eagerly in advance of the heavy-laden canoes. Grim news met him soon after he reached Fort St. Charles on the Lake of the Woods. His nephew La Jemeraye, a born leader of men, who was at the most advanced station, Fort Maurepas on Lake Winnipeg, had broken down from exposure, anxiety, and overwork, and had been laid in a lonely grave in the wilderness. Nearly all pioneer work is a record of tragedy and its gloom lies heavy on the career of La Vérendrye. A little later came another sorrow-laden disaster. La Vérendrye sent his eldest son Jean back to Rainy Lake to hurry the canoes from Montreal which were bringing needed food. The

party landed on a peninsula at the discharge of
Rainy Lake into Rainy River, fell into an ambush
of Sioux Indians, and were butchered to a man.
This incident reveals the chief cause of the slow
progress in discovery in the Great West: the temper of the savages was always uncertain.

There is no sign that La Vérendrye wavered in
his great hope even when he realized that the
Winnipeg River was not the river flowing westward which he sought. We know now that the
northern regions of the American continent east
of the Rocky Mountains are tilted towards the
east and the north and that in all its vast spaces
there is no great river which flows to the west.
La Vérendrye, however, ignorant of this dictate
of nature, longed to paddle with the stream towards the west. The Red River flows from the
south into Lake Winnipeg at a point near the
mouth of the Winnipeg River. Up the Red River
went La Vérendrye and found a tributary, the
Assiniboine, flowing into it from the west. At the
point of junction, where has grown up the city of
Winnipeg, he built a tiny fort, called Fort Rouge,
a name still preserved in a suburb of the modern
Winnipeg. The explorers went southward on the
Red River, and then went westward on the Assini-

boine River only to find the waters persistently flowing against them and no definite news of other waters leading to the Western Sea. On the Assiniboine, near the site of the present town of Portage la Prairie in Manitoba, La Vérendrye built Fort La Reine. Its name is evidence still perhaps of hopes for aid through the Queen if not through the King of France.

In 1737 La Vérendrye made once more the long journey to Montreal. His fourteen canoes laden with furs were an earnest of the riches of the wonderful West and so pleased his Montreal partners that again they fitted him out with adequate supplies. In the summer of 1738 we find him at Fort La Reine, rich for the moment in goods with which to trade, keen and competent as a trader, and having great influence with the natives. All through the West he found Indians who went to trade with the English on Hudson Bay, and he constantly urged them not to take the long journey but to depend upon the French who came into their own country. It was a policy well fitted to cause searching of heart among the English traders who seemed so secure in their snug quarters on the seashore waiting for the Indians to come to them.

La Vérendrye had now a fresh plan for penetrating farther on his alluring quest. He had heard of a river to the south to be reached by a journey overland. It was a new thing for him to abandon canoes and march on foot but this he now did and with winter approaching. On October 16, 1738, when the autumn winds were already chill, there was a striking little parade at Fort La Reine. The drummer beat the garrison to arms. What with soldiers brought from Canada, the voyageurs who had paddled the great canoes, and the Indians who dogged always the steps of the French traders, there was a muster at the fort of some scores of men. La Vérendrye reviewed the whole company and from them chose for his expedition twenty soldiers and voyageurs and about twenty Assiniboine Indians. As companions for himself he took François and Pierre, two of his three surviving sons, and two traders who were at the fort.

We can picture the little company setting out on the 18th of October on foot, with some semblance of military order, by a well-beaten trail leading across the high land which separates the Red River country from the regions to the southwest. La Vérendrye had heard much of a people, the Mandans, dwelling in well-ordered villages on the banks of a great river and cultivating the soil instead of living the wandering life of hunters. Such wonders of Mandan culture had been reported to La Vérendrye that he half expected to find them white men with a civilization equal to that of Europe. The river was in reality not an unknown stream, as La Vérendrye hoped, but the Missouri, a river already frequented by the French in its lower stretches where its waters join those of the Mississippi.

It was a long march over the prairie. La Vérendrye found that he could not hurry his Indian guides. They insisted on delays during days of glorious autumn weather when it would have been wise to press on and avoid the winter cold on the wind-swept prairie. They went out of their way to visit a village of their own Assiniboine tribe; and, when they resumed their journey, this whole village followed them. The prairie Indians had a more developed sense of order and discipline than the tribes of the forest. La Vérendrye admired the military regularity of the savages on the march. They divided the company of more than six hundred into three columns: in front, scouts to look out for an enemy and also for herds of buffalo; in the center, well protected, the old and the lame, all those incapable of fighting; and, for a rear-guard, strong fighting men. When buffalo were seen, the most active of the fighters rushed to the front to aid in hemming in the game. Women and dogs carried the baggage, the men condescending to bear only their weapons.

Not until cold December had come did the party reach the chief Mandan village. It was in some sense imposing, for the Indian lodges were arranged neatly in streets and squares and the surrounding palisade was strong and well built. Around the fort was a ditch fifteen feet deep and of equal width, which made the village impregnable in Indian warfare. After saluting the village with three volleys of musket fire, La Vérendrye marched in with great ceremony, under the French flag, only to discover that the Mandans were not greatly unlike the Assiniboines and other Indians of the West whom he already knew. The men went about naked and the women nearly so. They were skilled in dressing leather. They were also cunning traders, for they duped La Vérendrye's friends, the Assiniboines, and cheated them out of their muskets, ammunition, kettles, and knives. Great eaters were the Mandans. They cultivated abundant crops and stored them in cave cellars. Every day they brought their visitors more than twenty dishes cooked in earthen pottery of their own handicraft. There was incredible feasting, which La Vérendrye avoided but which his sons enjoyed. The Mandan language he could not understand and close questioning as to the route to the Western Sea was thus impossible. He learned enough to discredit the vague tales of white men in armor and peopled towns with which his lying guides had regaled him. In the end he decided for the time being to return to Fort La Reine and to leave two of his followers to learn the Mandan language so that in the future they might act as interpreters. When he left the Mandan village on the 13th of December, he was already ill and it is a wonder that he did not perish from the cold on the winter journey across hill and prairie. "In all my life I have never," he says, "endured such misery from illness and fatigue, as on that journey." On the 11th of February he was back at Fort La Reine, worn out and broken in health but still undaunted and resolved never to abandon his search.

Abandon it he never did. We find him in Montreal in 1740 involved in what he had always held in horror — a lawsuit brought against him by some impatient creditor. The report had gone abroad that he was amassing great wealth, when, as he said, all that he had accumulated was a debt of forty thousand *livres*. In the autumn of 1741 he was back at Fort La Reine, where he welcomed his son Pierre from a fruitless journey to the Mandans.

The most famous of all the efforts of the family was now on foot. On April 29, 1742, a new expedition started from Fort La Reine, led by La Vérendrye's two sons, Pierre and François. They knew the nature of the task before them, its perils as well as its hopes. They took with them no imposing company as their father had done, but only two men. The party of four, too feeble to fight their way, had to trust to the peaceful disposition of the natives. When they started, the prairie was turning from brown to green and the rivers were still swollen from the spring thaw. In three weeks they reached a Mandan village on the upper Missouri and were well received. It was after midsummer when they set out again and pressed on westward with a trend to the south. The country was bare and desolate. For twenty days they saw no human being. They had Mandan guides who promised to take them to the next tribe, the Handsome Men — *Beaux Hommes* — as the brothers called them, a tribe much feared by the Mandans. The travelers were now mounted; for the horse, brought first to America by the Spaniards, had run wild on the western plains where the European himself had not yet penetrated, and had become an indispensable aid to certain of the native tribes. Deer and buffalo were in abundance and they had no lack of food.

When they reached the tribe of *Beaux Hommes*, the Mandan guides fled homeward. Summer passed into bleak autumn with chill winds and long nights. By the end of October they were among the Horse Indians who, they had been told, could guide them to the sea. These, however, now said that only the Bow Indians, farther on, could do this. Winter was near when they were among these Indians, probably a tribe of the Sioux, whom they found excitedly preparing for a raid on their neighbors farther west, the Snakes. They were going, they said, towards the mountains and there the Frenchmen could look out on the great sea. So the story goes on. The brothers advanced ever westward and the land became more rugged, for they were now climbing upward from the prairie country. At last, on January 1, 1743, they saw what both cheered and discouraged them. In the distance were mountains. About them was the prairie, with game in abundance. It was a great host with which the brothers traveled for there were two thousand warriors with their families who made night vocal with songs and yells. On the 12th of January, nearly two weeks later, with an advance party of warriors, the La Vérendryes reached the foot of the mountains, "well wooded with timber of every kind and very high."

Was it the Rocky Mountains which they saw? Had they reached that last mighty barrier of snow-capped peaks, rugged valleys, and torrential streams, beyond which lay the sea? That they had done so was long assumed and many conjectures have been offered as to the point in the Rockies near which they made their last camp. Their further progress was checked by an unexpected crisis. One day they came upon an encampment of the dreaded Snake Indians which had been abandoned in great haste. This, the Bow Indians thought, could only mean that the Snakes had hurriedly left their camp in order to slip in behind the advance guard of the Bows and massacre the women and children left in the rear. Panic seized the Bows and they turned homeward in wild confusion. Their chief could not restrain them. "I was very much disappointed," writes one of the brothers, "that I could not climb the mountains" — those mountains from which he had been told that he might view the Western Sea.

There was nothing for it but to turn back through snowdrifts over the bleak prairie. The progress was slow for the snow was sometimes two feet deep. On the 1st of March the brothers parted with their Bow friends at their village and then headed for home. By the 20th they were encamped with a friendly tribe on the banks of the Missouri. Here, to assert that Louis XV was lord of all that country, they built on an eminence a pyramid of stones and in it they buried a tablet of lead with an inscription which recorded the name of Louis XV, their King, and of the Marquis de Beauharnois, Governor of Canada, and the date of the visit.

Truth is sometimes stranger than fiction. One hundred and seventy years later, on February 16, 1913, a schoolgirl strolling with some companions on a Sunday afternoon near the High School in the town of Pierre, South Dakota, stumbled upon a projecting corner of this tablet, which was in an excellent state of preservation. Thus we know exactly where the brothers La Vérendrye were on April 2, 1743, when they bade farewell to their Indian friends and set out on horseback for Fort La Reine.

Spring had turned to summer before the brothers reached their destination. On July 2, 1743, they relieved the anxiety of their waiting father after an absence of fifteen months. Moving slowly as they did, could they have traveled from the distant Rockies from the time in January when they turned back? It seems doubtful; and in spite of the long-cherished belief that the brothers reached the foothills of the Rocky Mountains, it may be that they had not penetrated beyond the barrier which we know as the Black Hills. The chance discovery of a forgotten plate by school children may in truth prove that, as late as in 1750, the Rocky Mountains had not yet been seen by white men and that the first vision of that mighty range was obtained much farther north in Canada.

After 1743 the French seem to have made no further efforts to reach the Western Sea by way of the Missouri. If in reality the brothers had not gone beyond the Black Hills in South Dakota, then their most important work appears to have

9

been done within what is now Canada, as discoverers of the Saskatchewan, the mighty river
which carries to far-distant Hudson Bay the
waters melted on the eastern slopes of the Rocky
Mountains. It was by this route up the Saskatchewan that fifty years later was solved the
tough and haunting problem of going over the
mountains to the Pacific Ocean. La Vérendrye
now ascended the Saskatchewan for some three
hundred miles to the forks where it divides into
two great branches. He was going deeper into
debt but he hoped always for help from the King.
It is pathetic to see today, on the map of that part
of western Canada which he and his sons explored,
a town, a lake, and a county called Dauphin, in
honor of the heir to the throne of France. No
doubt La Vérendrye had the thought that some
day he might plead with the Dauphin when he
had become King for help in his great task.

Before the year 1749 had ended La Vérendrye,
who had returned to Montreal, was in his grave.
His sons, partners in his work, expected to be
charged with the task — to which the King, in
1749, had anew appointed their father — of con-
tinuing the work of discovery in the West. François, for a time ill, wrote in 1750 from Montreal to

La Jonquière, the Governor at Quebec, that he hoped to take up the plans of his father. The Governor's reply was that he had appointed another officer, Legardeur de Saint-Pierre, to lead in the search for the Western Sea. François hurried to Quebec. The Governor met him with a bland face and seemed friendly. François urged that he and his brothers claimed no preëminence and that they were ready to serve under the orders of Saint-Pierre. The Governor was hesitant; but at last told François frankly that the new leader desired no help either from him or from his brothers. François was dismayed. He and his brothers were in debt. Already he had sent on stores and men to the West and the men were likely to starve if not followed by provisions. His chief property was in the West in the form of goods which would be plundered without his guardianship. To tide over the immediate future he sold the one small piece of land in Montreal which he had inherited from his father and threw this slight sop to his urgent creditors.

Saint-Pierre, strong in his right of monopoly, insisted that the brothers should not even return to the West. François urged that to go was a matter of life and death. In some way he secured leave to set out with one laden canoe. When Saint-Pierre found that François had gone, he claimed damages for the intrusion on his monopoly and secured an order to pursue François and bring him back. He caught him at Michilimackinac. The meeting between the two men at that place involved explanations. Face to face with an injured man, Saint-Pierre admitted that he had been in the wrong, paid to François many compliments, and regretted that he had not joined hands with the brothers.

The mischief done was, however, irreparable. François, crippled by opposition, could not carry on his trade with success and in the end he returned to Montreal a ruined man overwhelmed with debt. He wrote to the French court a noble appeal for relief:

I remain without friends and without patrimony . . . a simple ensign of the second grade; my elder brother has only the same rank as myself; my younger brother is only a junior cadet. This is the result of all that my father, my brothers and myself have done. . . . There are in the hands of your Lordship resources of compensation and of consolation. I venture to appeal to you for relief. To find ourselves excluded from the West would mean to be cruelly robbed of our heritage, to realize for ourselves all that is bitter and to see others secure all that is sweet.

The appeal fell on deaf ears. The brothers sank into obscurity. During Montcalm's campaigns from 1756 to 1759 Pierre and François seem to have been engaged in military service. François was killed in the siege of Quebec in 1759. After the final surrender of Canada the *Auguste*, a ship laden for the most part with refugees returning to France, was wrecked on the St. Lawrence. Among those on board who perished was Pierre de la Vérendrye. He died amid the howling of the tempest and the cries of drowning men. Tragedy, unrelenting, had pursued him to the end.

Legardeur de Saint-Pierre, the choice of the Marquis de la Jonquière to take up the search for the Western Sea in succession to the elder La Vérendrye, himself went only as far as Fort La Reine. It was a subordinate, the Chevalier de Niverville, whom he sent farther west to find the great mountains and if possible the sea. The winter of 1750–51 had set in before Niverville was ready. He started apparently from Fort Maurepas, on snowshoes, his party dragging their supplies on toboggans. Before they reached Paskoya on the Saskatchewan (the modern Le Pas) they had nearly perished of hunger and were able to save

their lives only by catching a few fish through the
ice. Niverville was ill. He sent forward ten men
by canoe up the Saskatchewan. They traveled
with such rapidity that on May 29, 1751, they
had reached the Rockies. They built a good fort,
which they named Fort La Jonquière, and stored
it with a considerable quantity of provisions. If,
as seems likely, the brothers La Vérendrye saw
only the Black Hills, these ten unknown men were
the discoverers of the Rocky Mountains.

Saint-Pierre braced himself to set out for the
distant goal but he was easily discouraged. Niverville, he said, was ill; the Indians were at war
among themselves; some of them were plotting
what Saint-Pierre calls "treason" to the French
and their "perfidy" surpassed anything in his life-
long experience. The hostile influence of the English he thought all-pervasive. Obviously these
are excuses. He did not like the task and he
turned back. As it was, he tells a dramatic story
of how Indians crowded into Fort La Reine in a
threatening manner and how he saved the fort
and himself only by rushing to the magazine with
a lighted torch, knocking open a barrel of powder,
and threatening to blow up everything and every-
body if the savages did not withdraw at once. He

was eager to leave the country. In 1752 he handed
over the command to St. Luc de la Corne and, in
August of that year, having experienced "much
wretchedness" on his journeys, he was safely back
in Montreal. The founding of Fort La Jonquière
was, no doubt, a great feat. Where the fort stood
we do not know. It may have been on the North
Saskatchewan, near Edmonton, or on the south
branch of the river near Calgary. In any case it
was a far-flung outpost of France.

The English had always been more prosaic than
the French. The traders on Hudson Bay worked,
indeed, under a monopoly not less rigorous than
that which Canada imposed. Without doubt,
many an Englishman on the Bay was haunted by
the hope and desire to reach the Western Sea.
But the servants of the Company knew that to
buy and sell at a profit was their chief aim. They
had been on the whole content to wait for trade
to come to them. By 1740 the Indians, who made
the long journey to the Bay by the intricate waters
which carried to the sea the flood of the Saskatchewan and Lake Winnipeg, were showing to the English articles supplied by the French at points far
inland. It thus became evident that the French

were tapping the traffic in furs near its source and cutting off the stream which had long flowed to Hudson Bay.

In June, 1754, Anthony Hendry, a young man in the service of the Company, left York factory on Hudson Bay to find out what the French were doing. We have a slight but carefully written diary of Hendry's journey. He does not fail to note that in the summer weather life was made almost intolerable by the "musketoos." Traveling by canoe he reached the Saskatchewan River and tells how, on the 22d of July, he came to "a French house." It was Fort Paskoya. When Hendry paddled up to the river bank two Frenchmen met him and "in a very genteel manner" invited him into their house. With all courtesy they asked him, he says, if he had any letter from his master and where and on what design he was going inland. His answer was that he had been sent "to view the Country" and that he intended to return to Hudson Bay in the spring. The Frenchmen were sorry that their own master, who was apparently the well-known Canadian leader, St. Luc de la Corne, the successor of Saint-Pierre, had gone to Montreal with furs, and added their regrets that they must detain Hendry until this leader's return. At this Hendry's Indians grunted and said that the French dared not do so. Next day Hendry took breakfast and dinner at the fort, gave "two feet of tobacco" (at that time it was sold in long coils) to his hosts, and in return received some moose flesh. The confidence of his Indian guides that the French would not dare to detain him was justified. Next day Hendry paddled on up the river and advanced more than twenty miles, camping at night by "the largest Birch trees I have yet seen."

Hendry wished to see the country thoroughly and to come into touch with the natives. The best way to do this and to obtain food was to leave the river and go boldly overland. He accordingly left his canoes behind and advanced on foot. The party was starving. On a Sunday in July he walked twenty-six miles and says "neither Bird nor Beast to be seen, — so that we have nothing to eat." The next day he traveled twenty-four miles on an empty stomach and then, to his delight, found a supply of ripe strawberries, "the size of black currants and the finest I ever eat." The next day his Indians killed two moose. He then met natives who, when he asked them to go to Hudson Bay to trade, replied that they could obtain all they needed from the French posts. The tact and skill of the French were such that, as Hendry admits, reluctantly enough, the Indians were already strongly attached to them. Day after day Hendry journeyed on over the rolling prairie in the warm summer days. He came to the south branch of the Saskatchewan near the point where now stands the city of Saskatoon and crossed the river on the 21st of August. Then on to the West, eager to take part in the hunting of the buffalo.

Hendry is almost certainly the first Englishman to see this region. In the end he reached the mountains. He makes no mention of having seen or heard anything of Fort La Jonquière, built three years earlier. He had aims different from those of La Vérendrye and other French explorers. Not the Western Sea but openings for trade was he seeking. His great aim was to reach the tribe called later the Blackfeet Indians, who were mighty hunters of the buffalo. Hendry was alive to the impressions of nature. The intense heat of August was followed in September by glorious weather, with the nights cool and the mosquitoes no longer troublesome. The climate was bracing. He complains only, from time to time, of swollen feet, and we need not wonder since his daily march occasionally went beyond twenty-five miles. Sometimes for days he saw no living creature. At other times wild life was prolific: there were moose in great abundance, bears, including the dreaded grizzly — one of which killed an Indian of his company and badly mutilated another — beaver, wild horses, and, above all, the buffalo. "Saw many herds of Buffalo grazing like English cattle," he says, on the 13th of September, and the next day he goes buffalo hunting. Guns and ammunition were costly. His Indians, who used only bows and arrows, on this day killed seven — "fine sport," says Hendry. Often the Indians took only the tongue, leaving the carcass for the wolves, who naturally abounded in such advantageous conditions. It is not easy now to imagine the part played by the buffalo in the life of the prairie. As Hendry advanced the herds were so dense as sometimes to retard his progress. Other writers tell of the vast numbers of these creatures. Alexander Henry, the younger, writing on April 1, 1801, says that in a river swollen by spring floods, drowned buffalo floated past his camp in one continuous line for two days and two nights. In prairie fires thousands were blinded and would go tumbling down banks into streams or lie down to die. One morning the bellowing of buffaloes awakened Henry and he looked out to see the prairie black. "The ground was covered at every point of the compass, as far as the eye could reach, and every animal was in motion."

Daily as Hendry advanced he saw smoke in the distance and his Indians told him that it came from the camp of the Blackfeet. He reached them on Monday the 14th of October. When four miles away he was stopped by mounted scouts who asked whether he came as a friend or as an enemy. He was taken to the camp of two hundred tents pitched in two rows, and was led through the long passage between the tents to the big tent of the chief of whom he had heard much. Not a word was spoken. The chief sat on a white buffalo skin. Pipes were passed round and each person was presented with boiled buffalo flesh. When talk began, Hendry told the chief that his great leader had sent him to invite them to come to trade at Hudson Bay where his people would get powder, shot, guns, cloth, beads, and other things. The chief said it was far away, and his people knew nothing of paddling. Such strangers to great waters were they that they would not even eat fish. They despised Hendry's tobacco. What they smoked was dried horse dung. In the end Hendry was dismissed and ordered to make his camp a quarter of a mile away from that of the Blackfeet.

It was close by the present site of Calgary and apparently in full view, on clear days, of the white peaks of the Rocky Mountains that Hendry visited the Blackfeet. He lingered in the far western country through the greater part of the winter. On a portion of his return journey he used a horse. When the spring thaw came, once more he took to the water in canoes. He complains of the idleness of his Indian companions who would remain in their huts all day and never stir to lay up a store of food even when game was abundant. Conjuring, dancing to the hideous pounding of drums, feasting and smoking, were their amusements. On his way back Hendry revisited the French post on the Saskatchewan. The leader, no doubt St. Luc de la Corne, had returned from Montreal and now had with him nine men. "The master," says Hendry, "invited me in to sup with him, and was very kind. He is dressed very Genteel." He showed Hendry his stock of furs; "a brave parcel," the admiring rival thought. Hendry admits the superiority of the French as traders. They "talk Several Languages to perfection; they have the advantage of us in every shape." In the West, as in the East, France was recognized as a formidable rival of England for the mastery of North America.

When Hendry was making his peaceful visit to the French fort in 1755, the crisis of the struggle had just been reached. In that year the battle line from Acadia to the Ohio and the Mississippi was already forming, and the fate of France's eager efforts to hold the West was soon to be decided in the East. If Britain should conquer on the St. Lawrence, she would conquer also on the Saskatchewan and on the Mississippi.

Conquer she did, and thus it happened that it was Britain's sons who took up the later burdens of the discoverer. In the summer of 1789, just at the time when the great Revolution was beginning in France, Alexander Mackenzie, a Scotch trader from Montreal, starting from Lake Athabasca, north of the farthest point reached by Hendry, was pressing still onward into an unknown region to find a river which might lead to the sea. This river he found; we know it now as the Mackenzie. For two weeks he and his Indians and voyageurs paddled with the current down this mighty stream, and on July 14, 1789, the day of the fall of the Bastille, he saw whales sporting in Arctic waters.

The real goal which Mackenzie sought was that of La Vérendrye, a western and not a northern ocean. Three years later, after months of preparation, he attempted the great feat of crossing the Rocky Mountains to the sea. After nine months of rugged travel, across mountain streams and gorges, in peril daily from hostile savages, on July 22, 1793, he reached the shore of the Pacific Ocean, the first white man to go by land over the width of the continent from sea to sea. It was thus a Scotchman who achieved that of which La Vérendrye had so long dreamed; and with no aid from the state but with only the resources of a trading company.

Ten years later, when France sold to the United States her last remaining territory of Louisiana, the American Government equipped an expedition under Lewis and Clark to cross the Rocky Mountains by way of the Missouri, the route from which the La Vérendrye brothers had been obliged to turn back. The party began the ascent of the Missouri on May 14, 1804, and arrived in the Mandan country in the late autumn. Here they spent the winter of 1804–05. Not until

November 15, 1805, had they completed the hard journey across the Rocky Mountains and reached the mouth of the Columbia River on the Pacific Ocean. Little did La Vérendrye, in his eager search for the Western Sea, imagine the difficulties to be encountered and the hardships to be endured by those who were destined, in later days, to realize his dream.

CHAPTER VI

THE VALLEY OF THE OHIO

ALMOST at the moment in 1749 when British ships were lying at anchor in Halifax harbor and sending to shore hundreds of boatloads of dazed and expectant settlers for the new colony, there had set out from Montreal, in the interests of France, an expedition with designs so far-reaching that we wonder still at the stupendous issues involved in efforts which seem so petty. The purpose of France was now to make good her claim to the whole vast West. It was a picturesque company which pushed its canoes from the shore at Lachine on the 15th of June, six days before the British squadron reached Halifax. There was a procession of twenty-three great birchbark canoes well filled, for in them were more than two hundred men, at least ten in each canoe, together with the necessary impedimenta for a long journey. There were twenty soldiers in uniform, a hundred and

eighty Canadians skilled in paddling and in carrying canoes and freight over the portages, a band
of Indians, and fourteen officers with Céloron de
Blainville at their head.

The acting Governor of Canada at this time
was a dwarf in physique, but a giant in intellect,
the brilliant naval officer, the Marquis de la
Galissonière, destined later to inflict upon the
English in the Mediterranean the naval defeat
which caused the execution of Admiral Byng as a
coward. This remarkable man — planning, like
his predecessor Frontenac, on a scale suited to
world politics — saw that the peace of 1748 settled
nothing, that in the balance now was the whole
future of North America, and that victory would
be to the alert and the strong. He chose Céloron,
the most capable of the hardy young Canadian
noblesse whom he had at hand, a man accustomed
to the life of the forest, and sent with him this
large party to assert against the English the right
of France to the valley of the Ohio. The English
were now to be shut out definitely from advancing
westward and to be confined to the strip of territory lying between the Atlantic coast and the Alle-
ghany Mountains, a little more than that strip
fifty miles wide talked about in Quebec as the

maximum concession of France, but still not very much according to the ideas of the English, and even this not secure if France should ever grow strong enough to crowd them out.

At no time do we find more vivid the contrast in type between the two nations. Before a concrete fact the British take action. When they gave up Louisbourg they built Halifax. Their traders had pressed into the Ohio country, not directed under any grandiose idea of empire, but simply as individuals, to trade and reap for themselves what profit they could. When they were checked and menaced by the French, they saw that something must be done. How they did it we shall see presently. It was the weakness of the English colonies that they could not unite to work out a great plan. If Virginia took steps to advance westward, Pennsylvania was jealous lest lands which she desired should go to a rival colony. France, on the other hand, had complete unity of design. Céloron spoke in the name of the King of France and he spoke in terms uncompromising enough. "The Ohio," said the King of France through his agent, "belongs to me." It is a French river. The lands bordering upon it are "my lands." The English intruders are foreign robbers and not one of them is to be left in the western country: "I will not endure the English on my land." The Indians, dwelling in that region, are "my children."

Scattered over the vast region about the Great Lakes were a good many French. At the lower end of Lake Ontario stood Fort Frontenac, a menace to the colony of New York, as the dwellers in the British post of Oswego on the opposite shore of the lake well knew. We have already seen that the French held a fort at Niagara guarding the route leading farther west to Lake Erie and to regions beyond Lake Erie, by way of the Ohio or the upper lakes, to the Mississippi. Near the mouth of the Mississippi, New Orleans was now becoming a considerable town with a governor independent of the governor at Quebec. Along the Mississippi at strategic points stretching northward beyond the mouth of the Missouri were a few French settlements, ragged enough and with a shiftless population of fur traders and farmers, but adequate to assert France's possession of that mighty highway. The weak point in France's position was in her connection of the Mississippi with the St. Lawrence by way of the Ohio. This was the place of danger, for here English rivalry was strongest, and it was to cure this weakness that Céloron was now sent forth.

Céloron moved toilsomely over the portage which led past the great cataract of Niagara and launched his canoes on Lake Erie. From its south shore, during seven days of heart-breaking labor, the party dragged the canoes and supplies through dense forest and over steep hills until they reached Chautauqua Lake, the waters of which flow into the Allegheny River and by it to the Ohio. For many weary days they went with the current, stopping at Indian villages, treating with the savages, who were sometimes awed and sometimes menacing. They warned the Indians to have no dealings with the scheming English who would "infallibly prove to be robbers," and asserted as boldly as Céloron dared the lordship of the King of France and his love for his forest children. Céloron realized that he was on an historic mission. At several points on the Ohio, with great ceremony, he buried leaden plates, as La Vérendrye had done a few years earlier in the far West, bearing an inscription declaring that, in the name of the King of France, he took possession of the country. On trees over these memorials of lead he nailed the arms of France, stamped on sheets of tin. Since that day at least three of the plates have been found.

Céloron's expedition went well enough. He advanced as far west on the Ohio as the mouth of the Great Miami River, then up that river, and by difficult portages back to Lake Erie. It was a remarkable journey; but in the late autumn he was back again in Montreal, not sure that he had achieved much. The natives of the country were, he thought, hostile to France and devoted to the English who had long traded with them. This opinion was in truth erroneous, for, when the time of testing came, the Indians of the West fought on the side of France. Montcalm had many hundreds of them under his banner. The expedition meant the definite and final throwing down of the gauntlet by France. With all due ceremony she had declared that the Ohio country was hers and that there she would allow no English to dwell.

Legardeur de Saint-Pierre could hardly have known, when he left the hard region of the Saskatchewan in 1752, that a year later he would be sent to protect another set of outposts of France in the West. In 1753 we find him in command of the French forces in the Ohio country. Céloron had been sent to Detroit. If Saint-Pierre had played his part feebly on the Saskatchewan, he was now made for a brief period one of the central figures in the opening act of a world drama. It is with a touch of emotion that we see on the stage, as the opponent of this not great Frenchman, the momentous figure of George Washington.

The fight for North America was now rapidly approaching its final phase in the struggle which we know as the Seven Years' War. During forty years, commissioners of the two nations had been trying to reach some agreement as to boundaries. Each side, however, made impossible demands. France claimed all the lands drained by the St. Lawrence and the Great Lakes and by the Mississippi and its tributaries — a claim which, if made good, would have carried her into the very heart of the colony of New York and would have given her also the mastery of the Ohio and the regions beyond. Britain claimed all the lands ever occupied by the Iroquois Indians, who had been recognized as British subjects by the Treaty of Utrecht. As those Indians had overrun regions north of the St. Lawrence, the British thus would become masters of a good part of Canada. Neither side was prepared for reasonable compromise. The sword was to be the final arbiter.

Events moved rapidly towards war. In 1753 Duquesne, the new Governor of Canada, sent more than a thousand men to build Fort Le Bœuf, on upper waters flowing to the Ohio and within easy reach of support by way of Lake Erie. In the next year the French were swarming in the Ohio Valley, stirring up the Indians against the English and confident of success. They jeered at the divisions among the English and believed their own unity so strong that they could master the colonies one by one. The two colonies most affected were Pennsylvania and Virginia, either of them quite ready to see its own citizens advance into the Ohio country and possess the land, but neither of them willing to unite with the other in effective military action to protect the frontier.

It is at this crisis that there appears for the first time in history George Washington of Virginia. In December, 1753, in the dead of winter, he made a long, toilsome journey from Virginia to the north through snow and rain, by difficult forest trails, over two ranges of mountains, across streams sometimes frozen, sometimes dangerous from treacherous thaws. On the way he heard gossip from the

Indians ab   out the designs of the French. They
boasted th   t they would come in numbers like the
sands of   e seashore; that the natives would be
no m   obstacle to them than the flies and
              which indeed they resembled; and that
mo   dth of a finger-nail of land belonged to
              . Washington was told by one of the
land   "it was their absolute design to take
old   of the Ohio and, by ——, they would do
              was no matter that the French were out-
              ered two to one by the English, for the Eng-
              n were dilatory and ineffective.

In the end, Washington arrived at Fort Le
Bœuf and presented a letter from Dinwiddie, the
Lieutenant-Governor of Virginia, pointing out
that the British could not permit an armed force
from Canada to invade their territory of the Ohio
and requiring that the French should leave the
country at once. Legardeur de Saint-Pierre, to
whom this firm demand was delivered, "an elderly
gentleman," says Washington, with "much the
air of a soldier" gave, of course, a polite answer in
the manner of his nation, but he intended, he said,
to remain where he was as long as he had instructions so to do. Washington kept his eyes open
and made careful observations of the plan of the

fort, the number of men, and also of th___ ___CE
which he noted that there were mor___ canoes, of
hundred ready and many others buil___ than two
French tried to entice away his Indian___ two
says, "I cannot say that ever in my life I The
so much anxiety." On the journey back he
perished when he fell into an ice-cold strea___
was obliged to spend the night on a tiny is___
in frozen clothing. He brought comfort as c___
to the waiting Dinwiddie.

The French meanwhile were always a littl___
ahead of the English in their planning. Early in
April, 1754, a French force of five or six hundred
men from Canada, which had set out while Quebec was still in the icy grip of winter, reached the
upper waters of the Ohio. They attacked and destroyed a fort which the English had begun at the
forks where now stands Pittsburgh, and, in its
place, began a formidable one, called Fort Duquesne after the Governor of Canada. In vain was
Washington sent with a few hundred men to take
possession of this fort and to assert the claim of the
English to the land. He fell in with a French
scouting party under young Coulon de Jumonville,
killed its leader and nine others, and took more
than a score of prisoners — warfare bloody enough

in a time of supposed peace. But the French were now on the Ohio in greater numbers than the English. At a spot known as the Great Meadows, where Washington had hastily thrown up defenses, which he called Fort Necessity, he was forced to surrender, but was allowed to lead his force back to Virginia, defeated in the first military adventure of his career. The French took the view that his killing of the young officer Jumonville was assassination, since no state of war existed, and raised a fierce clamor that Washington was a murderer — a strange contrast to his relations with France in the years to come.

What astonishes us in regard to these events is that Britain and France long remained nominally at peace while they were carrying on active hostilities in America and sending from Europe armies to fight. There were various reasons for this hesitation about plunging formally into war. Each side wished to delay until sure of its alliances in Europe. During the war ending in 1748 France had fought with Frederick of Prussia against Austria, and Britain had been Austria's ally. The war had been chiefly a land war, but France had been beaten on the sea. Now Britain and Prussia were drawing together and, if France fought them, it must be with Austria as an ally.   Such an alliance offered France but slight advantage.   Austria, an inland power, could not help France against an adversary whose strength was on the sea; she could not aid the designs of France in America or in India, where the capable French leader Dupleix was in a fair way to build up a mighty oriental empire.   Nor had France anything to gain in Europe from an Austrian alliance.   The shoe was on the other foot. The supreme passion of Maria Theresa who ruled Austria was to recover the province of Silesia which had been seized in 1740 by Prussia and held — held to this day.   Austria could do little for France but France could do much for Austria. So Austria worked for this alliance.   It is a story of intrigue.   Usually in France the King carried on negotiations with foreign countries only through his ministers, who knew the real interests of France. Now the astute Austrian statesman, Kaunitz, went past the ministers of Louis XV to Louis himself.   This was the heyday of Madame de Pompadour, the King's mistress.   Maria Theresa condescended to intrigue with this woman whom in her heart she despised.   There is still much mystery in the affair.   The King was flattered into thinking that personally he was swaying the affairs of Europe and took delight in deceiving his ministers and working behind their backs. While events in America were making war between France and Britain inevitable, France was being tied to an ally who could give her little aid. She must spend herself to fight Austria's battles on the land, while her real interests required that she should build up her fleet to fight on the sea the great adversary across the English Channel.

The destiny of North America might, indeed, well have been other than it is. A France strong on the sea, able to bring across to America great forces, might have held, at any rate, her place on the St. Lawrence and occupied the valleys of the Ohio and the Mississippi. We can hardly doubt that the English colonies, united by a common deadly peril, could have held against France most of the Atlantic coast. But she might well have divided with them North America; and today the lands north of the Ohio and westward beyond the Ohio to the Pacific Ocean might have been French. The two nations on the brink of war in 1754 were playing for mighty stakes; and victory was to the power which had control of the sea. France had a great army, Britain a great fleet. In this contrast lay wrapped the secret of the future of North America.

As the crisis drew near the vital thought about the future of America was found, not in America, but in Europe. The English colonies were so accustomed to distrust each other that, when Virginia grew excited about French designs on the Ohio, Pennsylvania or North Carolina was as likely as not to say that it was the French who were in the right and a stupid, or excitable, or conceited, colonial governor who was in the wrong. In Paris and London, on the other hand, there were no illusions about affairs in America. In both capitals it was realized that a grim fight was on. During the winter of 1754–55 extensive preparations were being made on both sides. France equipped an army under Baron Dieskau to go to Canada; Britain equipped one under General Braddock to go to Virginia. Each nation asked the other why it was sending troops to America and each gave the assurance of benevolent designs. But in the spring of 1755 a British fleet under Admiral Boscawen put to sea with instructions to capture any French vessels bound for North America. At the same time the two armies were on the way across the Atlantic. Dieskau went to

Canada, Braddock to Virginia, each instructed to attack the other side, while in the meantime ambassadors at the two courts gave bland assurances that their only thought was to preserve peace.

The English colonists showed a political blindness that amounted to imbecility. Albany was the central point from which the dangers on all sides might best be surveyed. Here came together in the summer of 1754 delegates from seven of the colonies to consider the common peril. The French were busy in winning, as they did, the support of the many Indian tribes of the West; and the old allies of the English, the Iroquois, were nervous for their own safety. The delegates to Albany, tied and bound by instructions from their Assemblies, had to listen to plain words from the savages. The one Englishman who, in dealing with the Indians, had tact and skill equal to that of Frontenac of old, was an Irishman, Sir William Johnson. To him the Iroquois made indignant protests that the English were as ready as the French to rob them of their lands. If we find a bear in a tree, they said, some one will spring up to claim that the tree belongs to him and keep us from shooting the bear. The French, they added, are at least men who are prepared to fight; you weak and unprepared English are like women and any day the French may turn you out. Benjamin Franklin told the delegates that they must unite to meet a common enemy. Unite, however, they would not. No one of them would surrender to a central body any authority through which the power of the King over them might be increased. The Congress — the word is full of omen for the future — failed to bring about the much-needed union.

In February, 1755, Braddock arrived in Virginia with his army, and early in May he was on his march across the mountains with regulars, militia, and Indians, to the number of nearly fifteen hundred men, to attack Fort Duquesne and to rid the Ohio Valley of the French. He knew little of forest warfare with its use of Indian scouts, its ambushes, its fighting from the cover of trees. On the 9th of July, on the Monongahela River, near Fort Duquesne, in a struggle in the forest against French and Indians he was defeated and killed. George Washington was in the fight and had to report to Dinwiddie the dismal record of what had happened. The frontier was aflame; and nearly all the Indians of the West, seeing the rising star, went over to the French. The power of France was, for the time, supreme in the heart of the continent. At that moment even far away in the lone land about the Saskatchewan, the English trader, Hendry, had to admit that the French knew better than the English how to attract the support of the savage tribes.

Meanwhile Dieskau had arrived at Quebec. In the colony of New York Sir William Johnson, the rough and cheery Irishman, much loved of the Iroquois, was gathering forces to attack Canada. Early in July, 1755, Johnson had more than three thousand provincial troops at Albany, a motley horde of embattled farmers, most of them with no uniforms, dressed in their own homespun, carrying their own muskets, electing their own officers, and altogether, from the strict soldier's point of view, a rabble rather than an army. To meet this force and destroy it if he could, Dieskau took to the French fort at Crown Point, on Lake Champlain, and southward from there to Ticonderoga at the head of this lake, some three thousand five hundred men, including his French regulars, some Canadians and Indians. Johnson's force lay at Fort George, later Fort William Henry, the most southerly point on Lake George. The names, given by Johnson himself, show how the dull Hanoverian kings and their offspring were held in honor by the Irish diplomat who was looking for favors at court. The two armies met on the shores of Lake George early in September and there was an all-day fight. Each side lost some two hundred men. Among those who perished on the French side was Legardeur de Saint-Pierre, who had escaped all the perils of the western wilderness to meet his fate in this border struggle. The honors of the day seem to have been with Johnson, for the French were driven off and Dieskau himself, badly wounded, was taken prisoner. That Johnson had great difficulty in keeping his savages from burning alive and then boiling and eating Dieskau and smoking his flesh in their pipes, in revenge for some of their chiefs killed in the fight, shows what an alliance with Indians meant.

There was small gain to the English from Johnson's success. He was too cautious to advance towards Canada; and, as winter came on, he broke up his camp and sent his men to their homes. The colonies had no permanent military equipment. Each autumn their forces were dissolved to be reorganized again in the following spring, a lame method of waging war.

For three years longer in the valley of the Ohio, as elsewhere, the star of France remained in the ascendant. It began to decline only when, farther east, on the Atlantic, superior forces sent out from England were able to check the French. During the summer of 1758, while Wolfe and Boscawen were pounding the walls of Louisbourg, seven thousand troops led by General Forbes, Colonel George Washington, and Colonel Henry Bouquet, pushed their way through the wilds beyond the Alleghanies and took possession of the Ohio. The French destroyed Fort Duquesne and fled. On the 25th of November the English occupied the place and named it "Pitts-Bourgh" in honor of their great war minister.

CHAPTER VII

THE EXPULSION OF THE ACADIANS

WE have now to turn back over a number of years to see what has been happening in Acadia, that oldest and most easterly part of New France which in 1710 fell into British hands. Since the Treaty of Utrecht in 1713 the Acadians had been nominally British subjects. But the Frenchman, hardly less than the Jew, is difficult of absorption by other racial types. We have already noted the natural aim of France to recover what she had lost and her use of the priests to hold the Acadians to her interests. The Acadians were secure in the free exercise of their religion. They had no secular leaders and few, if any, clergy of their own. They were led chiefly by priests, subjects of France, who, though working in British territory, owned no allegiance to Great Britain, and were directed by the Bishop of Quebec.

For forty years the question of the Acadians

remained unsettled. Under the Treaty of 1713 the Acadians might leave the country. If they remained a year they must become British subjects. When, however, in 1715, two years after the conclusion of the treaty, they were required to take the oath of allegiance to the new King, George I, they declared that they could not do so, since they were about to move to Cape Breton. When George II came to the throne in 1727, the oath was again demanded. Still, however, the Acadians were between two fires. Their Indian neighbors, influenced by the French, threatened them with massacre if they took the oath, while the British declared that they would forfeit their farms if they refused. The truth is that the British did not wish to press the alternative. To drive out the Acadians would be to strengthen the neighboring French colony of Cape Breton. To force on them the oath might even cause a rising which would overwhelm the few English in Nova Scotia. So the tradition, never formally accepted by the British, grew up that, while the Acadians owed obedience to George II, they would be neutral in case of war with France. A common name for them used by the British themselves was that of the Neutral French. In time of peace the Acadians could be left to themselves. When, however, war broke out between Britain and France the question of loyalty became acute. Such war there was in 1744. Without doubt, some Acadians then helped the French — but it was, as they protested, only under compulsion and, as far as they could, they seem to have refused to aid either side. The British muttered threats that subjects of their King who would not fight for him had no right to protection under British law. Even then feeling was so high that there was talk of driving the Acadians from their farms and setting them adrift; and these poor people trembled for their own fate when the British victors at Louisbourg in 1745 removed the French population to France. Assurances came from the British government, however, that there was no thought of molesting the Acadians.

With the order "As you were" the dominant thought of the Treaty of Aix-la-Chapelle in 1748, the highly organized and efficient champions of French policy took every step to ensure that in the next struggle the interests of France should prevail. Peace had no sooner been signed than Versailles was working in Nova Scotia on the old policy. The French priests taught that eternal perdition awaited the Catholic Acadians who should accept the demands of the heretic English. The Indians continued their savage threats. Blood is thicker than water and no doubt the natural sympathies of the Acadians were with the French. But the British were now formidable. For them the founding of Halifax in 1749 had made all the difference. They, too, had a menacing fortress at the door of the Acadians, and their tone grew sterner. As a result the Acadians were told that if, by October 15, 1749, they had not taken an unconditional oath of allegiance to George II, they should forfeit their rights and their property, the treasured farms on which they and their ancestors had toiled. The Acadians were in acute distress. If they yielded to the English, not only would their bodies be destroyed by the savage Micmac Indians, but their immortal souls, they feared, would be in danger.

The Abbé Le Loutre was the parish priest of the Acadian village of Beaubassin on Chignecto Bay and also missionary to the Micmac Indians, whose chief village lay in British territory not many miles from Halifax. British officials of the time denounced him as a determined fanatic who did not stop short of murder. As in most men, there was in Le Loutre a mingling of qualities. He was arrogant, domineering, and intent on his own plans. He hated the English and their heresy, and he preached to his people against them with frantic invective. He incited his Indians to bloodshed. But he also knew pity. The custom of the Indians was to consider prisoners taken by them as their property, and on one occasion Le Loutre himself paid ransom to the Indians for thirtyseven English captives and returned them to Halifax. It is certain that the French government counted upon the influence of French priests to aid its political designs. "My masters, God and the King" was a phrase of the Sulpician father Piquet working at this time on the St. Lawrence. Le Loutre could have echoed the words. He was an ardent politician and France supplied him with both money and arms to induce the Indians to attack the English. The savages haunted the outskirts of Halifax, waylaid and scalped unhappy settlers, and, in due course, were paid from Louisbourg according to the number of scalps which they produced. The deliberate intention was to make new English settlements impossible in Nova Scotia and so to discourage the English that they should abandon Halifax. All this intrigue occurred in 1749 and the years following the treaty of peace. If the English suffered, so did the Acadians. Le Loutre told them that if once they became British subjects they would lose their priests and find their religion suppressed. Acadians who took the oath would, he said, be denied the sacraments of the Church. He would also turn loose on the offenders the murderous savages whom he controlled. If pressed by the English, the Acadians, rather than yield, must abandon their lands and remove into French territory.

At this point arises the question as to what were the limits of this French territory. In yielding Acadia in 1713, France had not defined its boundaries. The English claimed that it included the whole region stretching northeastward to the Gulf of St. Lawrence from the frontier of New England. The French, however, said that Acadia meant only the peninsula of Nova Scotia ending at the isthmus between Baie Verte and the Bay of Chignecto; and for years a Canadian force stood there on guard, daring the British to put a foot on the north side of the little river Missaguash, which the French said was the international boundary.

There was much excitement among the Acadians in 1750, when an English force landed on the isthmus and proceeded to throw up defenses on the south side of the river. This outpost, which in due time became Fort Lawrence, was placed on what even the French admitted to be British territory. Forthwith on a hill two or three miles away, on the other side of the supposed boundary, the French built Fort Beauséjour. Le Loutre was on the spot, blustering and menacing. He told his Acadian parishioners of the little village of Beaubassin, near Fort Lawrence and within the British area, that rather than accept English rule they must now abandon their lands and seek the protection of the French at Fort Beauséjour. With his own hands he set fire to the village church. The houses of the Acadians were also burned. A whole district was laid waste by fire. Women and children suffered fearful privations — but what did such things matter in view of the high politics of the priest and of France?

During four or five years the hostile forts confronted each other. In time of peace there was war. The French made Beauséjour a solid fort, for it still stands, little altered, though it has been abandoned for a century and a half. It was chiefly the Acadians, nominal British subjects, who built these thick walls.

The arrogant Micmacs demanded that the British should hand over to them the best half of Nova Scotia, and they emphasized their demand by treachery and massacre. One day a man, in the uniform of a French officer, followed by a small party, approached Fort Lawrence, waving a white flag. Captain Howe with a small force went out to meet him. As this party advanced, Indians concealed behind a dike fired and killed Howe and eight or ten others. Such ruses were well fitted to cause among the English a resolve to enforce severe measures. The fire burned slowly but in the end it flamed up in a cruel and relentless temper. French policy, too, showed no pity. The Governor of Canada and the colonial minister in France were alike insistent that the English should be given no peace and cared nothing for the sufferings of the unhappy Acadians between the upper and the nether millstone.

At last, in 1755, the English accomplished something decisive. They sent an army to Fort Lawrence, attacked Fort Beauséjour, forced its timid commander Vergor to surrender, mastered the whole surrounding country, and obliged Le Loutre himself to fly to Quebec. There he embarked for France. The English captured him on the sea, however, and the relentless and cruel priest spent many years in an English prison. His later years, when he reached France, do him some credit. By that time the Acadians had been driven from their homes. There were nearly a thousand exiles in England. Le Loutre tried to befriend these helpless people and obtained homes for some of them in the parish of Belle-Isle-en-Mer in France.

In the meantime the price of Le Loutre's intrigues and of the outrages of the French and their Indian allies was now to be paid by the unhappy Acadians. During the spring and summer of 1755, the British decided that the question of allegiance should be settled at once, and that the Acadians must take the oath. There was need of urgency. The army at Fort Lawrence which had captured Fort Beauséjour was largely composed of men from New England, and these would wish to return to their homes for the winter. If the Acadians remained and were hostile, the country thus occupied at laborious cost might quickly revert to the French. Already many Acadians had fought on the side of the French and some of them, disguised as Indians, had joined in savage outrage. A French fleet and a French army were reported as likely to arrive before the winter. In fact, France's naval power with its base at Louisbourg was still stronger than that of Britain with its base at Halifax. When the Acadians were told in plain terms that they must take the oath of allegiance, they firmly declined to do so without certain limitations involving guarantees that they should not be arrayed against France. The Governor at Halifax, Major Charles Lawrence, was a stern, relentless man, without pity, and his mind was made up. Shirley, Governor of Massachusetts, was in touch with Lawrence. The Acadians should be deported if they would not take the oath. This step, however, the government at London never ordered. On the contrary, as late as on August 13, 1755, Lawrence was counseled to act with caution, prudence, and tact in dealing with the "Neutrals," as the Acadians are called even in this official letter. Meanwhile, without direct warrant from London, Lawrence and his council at Halifax had taken action. His reasoning was that of a direct soldier. The Acadians would not take the full oath of British citizenship. Very well. Quite obviously they could not be trusted. Already they had acted in a traitorous way. Prolonged war with France was imminent. Since Acadians who might be allied with the savages could attack British posts, they must be removed. To replace them, British settlers could in time be brought into the country.

The thing was done in the summer and autumn of 1755. Colonel Robert Monckton, a regular officer, son of an Irish peer, who always showed an ineffable superiority to provincial officers serving under him, was placed in charge of the work. He ordered the male inhabitants of the neighborhood of Beauséjour to meet him there on the 10th of August. Only about one-third of them came — some four hundred. He told them that the government at Halifax now declared them rebels. Their lands and all other goods were forfeited; they themselves were to be kept in prison. Not yet, however, was made known to them the decision that they were to be treated as traitors of whom the province must be rid. No attempt was made anywhere to distinguish loyal from disloyal Acadians. Lawrence gave orders to the military officers to clear the country of all Acadians, to get them by any necessary means on board the transports which would carry them away, and to burn their houses and crops so that those not caught might perish or be forced to surrender during the coming winter. At the moment, the harvest had just been reaped or was ripening.

When the stern work was done at Grand Pré, at Pisiquid, now Windsor, at Annapolis, there were harrowing scenes. In command of the work at Grand Pré was Colonel Winslow, an officer from Massachusetts — some of whose relatives twenty-five years later were to be driven, because of their loyalty to the British King, from their own homes in Boston to this very land of Acadia. Winslow issued a summons in French to all the male inhabitants, down to lads of ten, to come to the church at Grand Pré on Friday, the 5th of September, to learn the orders he had to communicate. Those who did not appear were to forfeit their goods. No doubt many Acadians did not understand the summons. Few of them could read and it hardly mattered to them that on one occasion a notice on the church door was posted upside down. Some four hundred anxious peasants appeared. Winslow read to them a proclamation to the effect that their houses and lands were forfeited and that they themselves and their families were to be deported. Five vessels from Boston lay at Grand Pré. In time more ships arrived, but chill October had come before Winslow was finally ready.

By this time the Acadians realized what was to happen. The men were joined by their families. As far as possible the people of the same village were kept together. They were forced to march to the transports, a sorrow-laden company, women carrying babes in their arms, old and decrepit people borne in carts, young and strong men dragging what belongings they could gather. Winslow's task, as he says, lay heavy on his heart and hands: "It hurts me to hear their weeping and wailing and gnashing of teeth." By the 1st of November he had embarked fifteen hundred unhappy people. His last ship-load he sent off on the 13th of December. The suffering from cold must have been terrible.

In all, from Grand Pré and other places, more than six thousand Acadians were deported. They were scattered in the English colonies from Maine to Georgia and in both France and England. Many died; many, helpless in new surroundings, sank into decrepit pauperism. Some reached people of their own blood in the French colony of Louisiana and in Canada. A good many returned from their exile in the colonies to their former home after the Seven Years' War had ended. Today their descendants form an appreciable part of the population of Nova Scotia, New Brunswick, and Prince Edward Island. The cruel act did one thing effectively: it made Nova Scotia safe for the British cause in the attack that was about to be directed against Canada.

CHAPTER VIII

THE VICTORIES OF MONTCALM

IN France's last, most determined, and most tragic struggle for North America, the noblest aspect is typified in the figure of Montcalm.

The circle of the King and his mistress at Versailles does not tell the whole story of France at this time. No doubt Madame de Pompadour made and unmade ministers, but behind the ministers was the great administrative system of France, with servants alert and efficient, and now chiefly occupied with military plans to defeat the great Frederick of Prussia. At the same time the intellect of France was busy with problems of science and was soon to express itself in the massive volumes of Diderot's *Encyclopædia*. The soldiers of France were preparing to fight on many battlefields. The best of them took little part in the debilitating pleasures of Versailles.

Louis Joseph, Marquis de Montcalm, was a

member of the ancient nobility of Languedoc, in
the south of France. He was a scholar, a soldier,
and a landowner. He could write a Latin inscription, fight a battle, and manage a farm — all with
excellence. His was a fruitful race. His wife had
borne him ten children, of whom six had survived.
He was sincerely religious, a family man, enjoying
quiet evenings at home. In his career, as no doubt
in that of many other French leaders of the time,
we find no lurid lights, no gay scenes at court —
nothing but simple and laborious devotion to duty.
Though a grand seigneur, Montcalm was poor.
His letters show that his mind was always much
occupied with family affairs, the need of economy,
the careers of his sons, his mill, his plantations.
He showed the minute care in management which
the French practise better than the English. In
1756 he was forty-four years of age, a soldier who
had campaigned in Germany, Bohemia, and Italy,
had known victory and defeat, had been a prisoner
in the hands of the Austrians, and had made a
reputation as a man fit to lead. He lived far from
court and went to Paris only rarely. It was this
quiet man who, on January 31, 1756, was summoned to Paris to head the military force about
to be sent to Canada. Dieskau was a captive in

English hands, and Montcalm was to replace
Dieskau.

Thus began that connection of Montcalm with
Canada which was destined three or four years
later to bring to him first victory and then defeat,
death, and undying fame. On receiving his appointment he went to Paris, thanked the King in
person for the honor done him, and was delighted
that his son, a mere boy, was given the rank and
pay of a colonel, one of the few abuses of court
favor which we find in his career. On March 26,
1756, Montcalm embarked at Brest with his staff.
War had not yet been declared, but already
Britain had captured some three hundred French
merchant ships, had taken prisoner nearly ten
thousand French sailors, and was sweeping from
the sea the fleets of France.

Owing to the fear of British cruisers, the voyage
of Montcalm had its excitements. As usual, however, France was earlier in the field than Britain,
who had in April no force ready for America which
could intercept Montcalm. The storms were
heavy, and on Easter Day, when Mass was cele-
brated, a sailor firm on his feet had to hold the
chalice for the officiating priest. On board there
were daily prayers, and always the service ended

with cries of "God save the King!" Some of the officers on board were destined to survive to a new era in France when there should be no more a king.

Montcalm had with him a capable staff and a goodly number of young officers, gay, debonair, thinking not of great political designs about America but chiefly of their own future careers in France, and facing death light-heartedly enough. Next to Montcalm in command was the Chevalier de Lévis, a member of a great French family and himself destined to attain the high rank of Marshal of France, and a capable though not a brilliant soldier, whose chief gift was tact and the art of managing men.   Third in command was the Chevalier de Bourlamaque, a quiet, reserved man, with no striking social gifts and in consequence not likely at first to make a good impression, though Montcalm, who was at the beginning a little doubtful of his quality, came in the end to rely upon him fully. The most brilliant man in all that company was the young Colonel de Bougainville, Montcalm's chief aide-de-camp. Though only twenty-seven years old he was already famous in the world of science and was destined to be still more famous as a great navigator, to live through the whole period of the French Revolution, and to die only on the eve of the fall of Napoleon. In 1756 he was too young and clever to be always prudent in speech. It is from his quick eye and eager pen that we learn much of the inner story of these last days of New France. Montcalm discusses frankly in his letters these and other officers, with whom he was on the whole well pleased. In his heart he could echo the words of Bougainville as he watched the brilliant spectacle of the embarkation at Brest: "What a nation is ours! Happy is he who leads and is worthy of it."

It was in this spirit of confidence that Montcalm faced the struggle in America. For him sad days were to come and his sunny, vivacious, southern temperament caused him to suffer keenly. At first, however, all was full of brilliant promise. So eager was he that, when his ships lay becalmed in the St. Lawrence some thirty miles below Quebec, he landed and drove to the city. It is the most beautiful country in the world, he writes, highly cultivated, with many houses, the peasants living more like the lesser gentry of France than like peasants, and speaking excellent French. He found the hospitality in Quebec such that a Parisian would be surprised at the profusion of good things of every kind. The city was, he thought, like the best type of the cities of France. The Canadian climate was healthgiving, the sky clear, the summer not unlike that of Languedoc, but the winter trying, since the severe weather caused the inhabitants to remain too much indoors. He described the Canadian ladies as witty, lively, devout, those of Quebec amusing themselves at play, sometimes for high stakes; those of Montreal, with conversation and dancing. He confessed that one of them proved a little too fascinating for his own peace of mind. The intolerable thing was the need to meet and pay court to the Indians whom the Governor, the Marquis de Vaudreuil, regarded as valuable allies. These savages, brutal, changeable, exacting, Montcalm from the first despised. It filled him with disgust to see them swarming in the streets of Montreal, sometimes carrying bows and arrows, their coarse features worse disfigured by war-paint and a gaudy headdress of feathers, their heads shaven, with the exception of one long scalp-lock, their gleaming bodies nearly naked or draped with dirty buffalo or beaver skins. What allies for a refined grand seigneur of France! It was a costly burden to feed them. Sometimes they made howling demands for brandy and for *bouillon*, by which they meant human blood. Many of them were cannibals. Once Montcalm had to give some of them, at his own cost, a feast of three oxen roasted whole. To his disgust, they gorged themselves and danced round the room shouting their savage war-cries.

The Governor of Canada, Pierre de Rigaud, Marquis de Vaudreuil, belonged to one of the most ancient families of France, related to that of Lévis. He had been born in Canada where his father was Governor for the long period of twenty-two years, from 1703 to 1725, and in his outlook and prejudices he was wholly of New France, with a passionate devotion to its people, and a deep resentment at any airs of superiority assumed by those who came from old France. A certain admiration is due to Vaudreuil for his championship of the Canadians and even of the savages of the land of his birth against officers of his own rank and caste who came from France. There was in Canada the eternal cleavage in outlook and manners between the Old World and the New, which is found in equal strength in New England, and which was one of the chief factors in causing the American Revolution. Vaudreuil, born at Quebec in 1698, had climbed the official ladder step by step until, in 1742, he had been made Governor of Louisiana, a post he held for three years. He succeeded the Marquis Duquesne as Governor of Canada in the year before Montcalm arrived. He meant well but he was a vain man, always a leading figure in the small society about him, and obsessed by a fussy self-importance. He was not clever enough to see through flattery. The Intendant Bigot, next to the Governor the most important man in Canada, an able and corrupt rascal, knew how to manage the Governor and to impose his own will upon the weaker man. Vaudreuil and his wife between them had a swarm of needy relatives in Canada, and these and other Canadians who sought favors from the Governor helped to sharpen his antagonism to the officers from France. Vaudreuil believed himself a military genius. It was he and not Montcalm who had the supreme military command, and he regarded as an unnecessary intruder this general officer sent out from France.

Now that Montcalm was come, Vaudreuil showed a malignant alertness, born of jealousy, to snub and check him. Outward courtesies were, of course, maintained. Vaudreuil could be bland and Montcalm restrained, in spite of his southern temperament, but their dispatches show the bitterness in their relations. The court of France encouraged not merely the leaders but even officers in subordinate posts to communicate to it their views. A voluble correspondence about affairs in Canada has been preserved. Vaudreuil himself must have tried the patience of the French ministers for he wrote at prodigious length, exalting his own achievements to the point of being ludicrous. At the same time he belittled everything done by Montcalm, complained that he was ruining the French cause in America, hinted that he was in league with corrupt elements in Canada, and in the end even went so far as to request his recall in order that the more pliant Lévis might be put in his place. The letters of Montcalm are more reserved. Unlike Vaudreuil, he never stooped to falsehood. He knew that he was under the orders of the Governor and he accepted the situation. When operations were on hand, Vaudreuil would give Montcalm instructions so ambiguous that if he failed he would be sure to get the discredit, while, if he succeeded, to Vaudreuil would belong the glory.

War is, at best, a cruel business. In Europe its predatory barbarity was passing away and there the lives of prisoners and of women and children were now being respected. Montcalm had been reared under this more civilized code, and he and his officers were shocked by what Vaudreuil regarded as normal and proper warfare. In 1756 the French had a horde of about two thousand savages, who had flocked to Montreal from points as far distant as the great plains of the West. They numbered more than thirty separate tribes or nations, as in their pride they called themselves, and each nation had to be humored and treated as an equal, for they were not in the service of France but were her allies. They expected to be consulted before plans of campaign were completed. The defeat of Braddock in 1755 had made them turn to the prosperous cause of France. Vaudreuil gave them what they hardly required — encouragement to wage war in their own way. The more brutal and ruthless the war on the English, he said, the more quickly would their enemies desire the kind of peace that France must have. The result was that the western frontiers of the English colonies became a hell of ruthless massacre. The savages attacked English settlements whenever they found them undefended. A pioneer might go forth in the morning to his labor and

return in the evening to find his house in ashes
and his wife and children lying dead with the
scalps torn from their heads as trophies of savage
prowess.

For years, until the English gained the upper
hand over the French, this awful massacre went
on. Hundreds of women and children perished.
Vaudreuil reported with pride to the French court
the number of scalps taken, and in his annals
such incidents were written down as victories.
He warned Montcalm that he must not be too
strict with the savages or some day they would
take themselves off and possibly go over to the
English and leave the French without indispensable allies. He complained of the lofty tone of
the French regular officers towards both Indians
and Canadians, and assured the French court that
it was only his own tact which prevented an open
breach.

Canada lay exposed to attack by three routes:
by Lake Ontario, by Lake Champlain, and by the
St. Lawrence and the sea. It was vital to control
the route to the West by Lake Ontario, vital to
keep the English from invading Canada by way of
Lake Champlain, vital to guard the St. Lawrence
and keep open communications with France.

Montcalm first directed his attention to Lake Ontario. Oswego, lying on the south shore, was a fort much prized by the English as a base from which they could attack the French Fort Frontenac on the north side of the lake and cut off Canada from the West. If the English could do this, they would redeem the failure of Braddock and possibly turn the Indians from a French to an English alliance.

The French, in turn, were resolved to capture and destroy Oswego. In the summer of 1756, they were busy drawing up papers and instructions for the attack. Montcalm wrote to his wife that he had never before worked so hard. He kept every one busy, his aide-de-camp, his staff, and his secretaries. No detail was too minute for his observation. He regulated the changes of clothes which the officers might carry with them. He inspected hospitals, stores, and food, and he even ordered an alteration in the method of making bread. He reorganized the Canadian battalions and in every quarter stirred up new activity. He was strict about granting leave of absence. Sometimes his working day endured for twenty hours — to bed at midnight and up again at four o'clock in the morning. He went with Lévis to Lake

Champlain to see with his own eyes what was going on there. Then he turned back to Montreal. The discipline among the Canadian troops was poor and he stiffened it, thereby naturally causing great offense to those who liked slack ways and hated to take trouble about sanitation and equipment. He held interminable conferences with his Indian allies. They were astonished to find that the great soldier of whom they had heard so much was so small in stature, but they noted the fire in his eye. He despised their methods of warfare and notes with a touch of irony that, while every other barbarity continues, the burning of prisoners at the stake has rather gone out of fashion, though the savages recently burned an English woman and her son merely to keep in practice.

Montcalm made his plans secretly and struck suddenly. In the middle of August, 1756, he surprised and captured Oswego and took more than sixteen hundred prisoners. Of these, in spite of all that he could do, his Indians murdered some. The blow was deadly. The English lost vast stores; and now the French controlled the whole region of the Great Lakes. The Indians were on the side of the rising power more heartily than ever, and the unhappy frontier of the English colonies was so harried that murderous savages ventured almost to the outskirts of Philadelphia. Montcalm caused a *Te Deum* to be sung on the scene of his victory at Oswego. In August he was back in Montreal where again was sung another joyous *Te Deum*. He wrote letters in high praise of some of his officers, especially of Bourlamaque, Malartic, and La Pause, the last "*un homme divin.*" Some of the Canadian officers, praised by Vaudreuil, he had tried and found wanting. "Don't forget," he wrote to Lévis, "that Mercier is a feeble ignoramus, Saint Luc a prattling boaster, Montigny excellent but a drunkard. The others are not worth speaking of, including my first lieutenant-general Rigaud." This Rigaud was the brother of Vaudreuil. When the Governor wrote to the minister, he, for his part, said that the success of the expedition was wholly due to his own vigilance and firmness, aided chiefly by this brother, "*mon frère,*" and Le Mercier, both of whom Montcalm describes as inept. Vaudreuil adds that only his own tact kept the Indian allies from going home because Montcalm would not let them have the plunder which they desired.

Montcalm struck his next blow at the English

on Lake Champlain. In July, 1757, he had eight
thousand men at Ticonderoga, at the northern end
of Lake George. Two thousand of these were
savages drawn from more than forty different
tribes — a lawless horde whom the French could
not control. A Jesuit priest saw a party of them
squatting round a fire in the French camp roasting
meat on the end of sticks and found that the meat
was the flesh of an Englishman. English prisoners,
sick with horror, were forced to watch this feast.
The priest's protest was dismissed with anger:
the savages would follow their own customs; let
the French follow theirs. The truth is that the
French had been only too successful in drawing the
savages to them as allies. They formed now one-
quarter of the whole French army. They were of
little use as fighters and probably, in the long run,
the French would have been better off without
them. If, however, Montcalm had caused them
to go, Vaudreuil would have made frantic protests,
so that Montcalm accepted the necessity of such
allies.

Each success, however, brought some new horrors at the hands of the Indians. Montcalm captured Fort William Henry, at the southern end of
Lake George, in August, a year after the taking

of Oswego. Fort William Henry was the most advanced English post in the direction of Canada. The place had been left weak, for the Earl of Loudoun, Commander-in-Chief of the British forces in America, was using his resources for an expedition against Louisbourg, which wholly failed. Colonel Monro, the brave officer in command at Fort William Henry, made a strong defense, but was forced to surrender. The terms were that he should march out with his soldiers and the civilians of the place, and should be escorted in safety to Fort Edward, about eighteen miles to the south. This time the savages surpassed themselves in treachery and savagery. They had formally approved of the terms of surrender, but they attacked the long line of defeated English as they set out on the march, butchered some of their wounded, and seized hundreds of others as prisoners. Montcalm did what he could and even risked his life to check the savages. But some fifty English lay dead and the whole savage horde decamped for Montreal carrying with them two hundred prisoners.

Montcalm burned Fort William Henry and withdrew to Ticonderoga at the north end of the lake. Why, asked Vaudreuil, had he not advanced

further south into English territory, taken Fort
Edward — weak, because the English were in a
panic — menaced Albany itself, and advanced
even to New York? Montcalm's answer was that
Fort Edward was still strong, that he had no
transport except the backs of his men to take
cannon eighteen miles by land in order to batter
its walls, and that his Indians had left him. Moreover, he had been instructed to hasten his operations and allow his Canadians to go home to
gather the ripening harvest so that Canada might
not starve during the coming winter. Vaudreuil
pressed at the French court his charges against
Montcalm and without doubt produced some effect. French tact was never exhibited with more
grace than in the letters which Montcalm received
from his superiors in France, urging upon him with
suave courtesy the need of considering the sensi-
tive pride of the colonial forces and of guiding
with a light rein the barbaric might of the Indian
allies. It is hard to imagine an English Secretary
of State administering a rebuke so gently and yet
so unmistakably. Montcalm well understood what
was meant. He knew that some intrigue had been
working at court but he did not suspect that the
Governor himself, all blandness and compliments

to his face, was writing to Paris voluminous attacks on his character and conduct.

In the next summer (1758) Montcalm won another great success. He lay with his forces at Ticonderoga. The English were determined to press into the heart of Canada by way of Lake Champlain. All through the winter, after the fall of Fort William Henry, they had been making preparations on a great scale at Albany. By this time Amherst and Wolfe were on the scene in America, and they spent this summer in an attack on Louisbourg which resulted in the fall of the fortress. On the old fighting ground of Lake Champlain and Lake George, the English were this year making military efforts such as the Canadian frontier had never before seen. William Pitt, who now directed the war from London, had demanded that the colonies should raise twenty thousand men, a number well fitted to dismay the timid legislators of New York and Pennsylvania. At Albany fifteen thousand men came marching in by detachments — a few of them regulars, but most of them colonial militia who, as soon as winter came on, would scatter to their homes. The leader was General Abercromby — a leader, needless to say, with good connections in England, but with no other qualification for high command.

On July 5, 1758, there was a sight on Lake George likely to cause a flutter of anxiety in the heart of Montcalm at Ticonderoga. In a line of boats, six miles long, the great English host came down the lake and, early on the morning of the sixth, landed before the fort which Montcalm was to defend. The soul of the army had been a brilliant young officer, Lord Howe, who shared the hardships of the men, washed his own linen at the brook, and was the real leader trusted by the inept Abercromby. It was a tragic disaster for the British that at the outset of the fight Howe was killed in a chance skirmish. Montcalm's chief defense of Ticonderoga consisted in a felled forest. He had cut down hundreds of trees and, on high ground in front of the fort, made a formidable *abbatis* across which the English must advance. Abercromby had four men to one of Montcalm. Artillery would have knocked a passage through the trunks of the trees which formed the *abbatis*. Abercromby, however, did not wait to bring up artillery. He was confident that his huge force could beat down opposition by a rapid attack, and he made the attack with all courage and persistence. But the troops could not work through the thicket of fallen trunks and, as night came on, they had to withdraw baffled. Next day Lake George saw another strange spectacle — a British army of thirteen thousand men, the finest ever seen hitherto in America, retreating in a panic, with no enemy in pursuit. Nearly two thousand English had fallen, while Montcalm's loss was less than four hundred. He planted a great cross on the scene of the fight with an inscription in Latin that it was God who had wrought the victory. All Canada had a brief period of rejoicing before the gloom of final defeat settled down upon the country.

CHAPTER IX

MONTCALM AT QUEBEC

THE rejoicing in Canada was brief. Before the end of the year the British were victorious at both the eastern and western ends of the long battle-line. Louisbourg had fallen in July; Fort Duquesne, in November. Fort Frontenac — giving command of Lake Ontario and, with it, the West — had surrendered to Bradstreet in August just after Montcalm's victory at Ticonderoga. The Ohio was gone. The great fortress guarding the gateway to the Gulf was gone. The next English attack would fall on Quebec. Montcalm had told Vaudreuil in the autumn, with vigorous precision, that the period of petty warfare, for taking scalps and burning houses, was past. It was time now to defend the main trunk of the tree and not the outer branches. The best Canadians should be incorporated into and trained in the battalions of regulars. The militia regiments themselves should be clothed and drilled like regular soldiers. Interior posts, such as Detroit, should be held by the smallest possible number of men. This counsel enraged Vaudreuil. Montcalm, he wrote, was trying to upset everything. Vaudreuil was certain that the English would not attack Quebec.

There is a melancholy greatness in the last days of Montcalm. He was fighting against fearful odds. With only about three thousand trained regulars and perhaps four times as many untrained Canadians and savages, he was confronting Britain's might on sea and land which was now thrown against New France. From France itself Montcalm knew that he had nothing to hope. In the autumn of 1758 he sent Bougainville to Versailles. That brilliant and loyal helper managed to elude the vigilance of the British fleet, reached Versailles, and there spent some months in varied and re-sourceful attempts to secure aid for Canada. He saw ministers. He procured the aid of powerful connections of his own and of his fellow-officers in Canada. He went to what was at this time the fountainhead of authority at the French court, and it was not the King. "The King is nothing," wrote Bougainville, "the Marchioness is all-power-ful — prime minister." Bougainville saw the

Marchioness, Madame de Pompadour, and read to her some of Montcalm's letters. She showed no surprise and said nothing — her habit, as Bougainville said. By this time the name of Montcalm was one to charm with in France. Bougainville wrote to him "I should have to include all France if I should attempt to give a list of those who love you and wish to see you Marshal of France. Even the little children know your name." There had been a time when the court thought the recall of Montcalm would be wise in the interests of New France. Now it was Montcalm's day and the desire to help him was real. France, however, could do little. Ministers were courteous and sympathetic; but as Berryer, Minister of Marine, said to Bougainville, with the house on fire in France, they could not take much thought of the stable in Canada.

This Berryer was an inept person. He was blindly ignorant of naval affairs, coarse, obstinate, a placeman who owed his position to intrigue and favoritism. His only merit was that he tried to cut down expenditure, but in regard to the navy this policy was likely to be fatal. It is useless, said this guardian of France's marine, to try to rival Britain on the sea, and the wise thing to do is to save money by not spending it on ships. Berryer even sold to private persons stores which he had on hand for the use of the fleet. If the house was on fire he did not intend, it would seem, that much should be left to burn. The old Duc de Belle-Isle, Minister of War, was of another type, a fine and efficient soldier. He explained the situation frankly in a letter to Montcalm. Austria was an exigent ally, and Frederick of Prussia a dangerous foe. France had to concentrate her strength in Europe. The British fleet, he admitted, paralyzed efforts overseas. There was no certainty, or even probability, that troops and supplies sent from France would ever reach Canada. France, the Duke said guardedly, was not without resources. She had a plan to strike a deadly blow against England and, in doing so, would save Canada without sending overseas a great army. The plan was nothing less than the invasion of England and Scotland with a great force, the enterprise which, nearly half a century later, Napoleon conceived as his master stroke against the proud maritime state. During that winter and spring France was building a great number of small boats with which to make a sudden descent and to land an army in England.

If this plan succeeded, all else would succeed.
Montcalm must just hold on, conduct a defensive
campaign and, above all, retain some part of Canada since, as the Duke said with prophetic fore-
sight, if the British once held the whole of the
country they would never give it up. Montcalm
himself had laid before the court a plan of his own.
He estimated that the British would have six men
to his one. Rather than surrender to them, he
would withdraw to the far interior and take his
army by way of the Ohio to Louisiana. The design was a wild counsel of despair for he would be
cut off from any base of supplies, but it shows the
risks he was ready to take. In him now the court
had complete confidence. Vaudreuil was instructed to take no military action without seeking the counsel of Montcalm. "The King," wrote
Belle-Isle to Montcalm, "relies upon your zeal,
your courage and your resolution." Some little
help was sent. The British control of the sea was
not complete; since more than twenty French ships
eluded British vigilance, bringing military stores,
food (for Canada was confronted by famine), four
hundred soldiers, and Bougainville himself, with a
list of honors for the leaders in Canada. Montcalm was given the rank of Lieutenant-General

and, but for a technical difficulty, would have been made a Marshal of France.

All this reliance upon Montcalm was galling to Vaudreuil. This weak man was entirely in the hands of a corrupt circle who recognized in the strength and uprightness of Montcalm their deadly enemy. An incredible plundering was going on. Its strength was in the blindness of Vaudreuil. The secretary of Vaudreuil, Grasset de Saint-Sauveur, an ignorant and greedy man, was a member of the ring and yet had the entire confidence of the Governor. The scale of the robberies was enormous. Bigot, the Intendant, was stealing millions of francs; Cadet, the head of the supplies department, was stealing even more. They were able men who knew how to show diligence in their official work. More than once Montcalm praises the resourcefulness with which Bigot met his requirements. But it was all done at a fearful cost to the State. Under assumed names the ring sold to the King, of whose interests they were the guardians, supplies at a profit of a hundred or a hundred and fifty per cent. They made vast sums out of transport. They drew pay for feeding hundreds of men who were not in the King's service. They received money for great bills of merchandise never delivered and repeated the process over and over again. To keep the Indians friendly the King sent presents of guns, ammunition, and blankets. These were stolen and sold. Even the bodies of Acadians were sold. They were hired out for their keep to a contractor who allowed them to die of cold and hunger. Hundreds of the poor exiles perished. The nemesis of a despotic system is that, however well-intentioned it may be, its officials are not controlled by an alert public opinion and yet must be trusted by their master. France meant well by her colony but the colony, unlike the English colonies, was not taught to look after itself. While nearly every one in Canada understood what was going on, it was another thing to inform those in control in France. La Porte, the secretary of the colonial minister, was in the service of the ring. He intercepted letters which should have made exposures. Until found out, he had the ear of the minister and echoed the tone of lofty patriotism which Bigot assumed in his letters to his superiors.

History has made Montcalm one of its heroes — and with justice. He was a remarkable man, who would have won fame as a scholar had he not followed the long family tradition of a soldier's

career. Bougainville once said that the highest
literary distinction of a Frenchman, a chair in the
Academy, might be within reach of Montcalm as
well as the baton of a Marshal of France. He had
a prodigious memory and had read widely. His
letters, written amid the trying conditions of war,
are nervous, direct, pregnant with meaning, the
notes of a penetrating intelligence. He had deep
family affection. "Adieu, my heart, I believe
that I love you more than ever I did before";
these were the last words of what he did not know
was to be his last letter to his wife. In the midst
of a gay scene at Montreal, in the spring of 1759,
he writes to Bourlamaque, then at Lake Champlain, with acute longing for the south of France in
the spring. For six or seven months in the year
he could receive no letters and always the British
command of the sea made their expected arrival
uncertain. "When shall I be again at the Château of Candiac, with my plantations, my oaks,
my oil mill, my mulberry trees? O good God."
He lays bare his spirit especially to Bourlamaque,
a quiet, efficient, thoughtful man, like himself, and
enjoins him to burn the letters — which he does
not, happily for posterity. Scandal does not touch
him but, like most Frenchmen, he is dependent

on the society of women.   He lived in a house on the ramparts of Quebec and visited constantly the *salons* of his neighbor in the Rue du Parloir, the beautiful and witty Madame de la Naudière.   In two or three other households he was also intimate and the Bishop was a sympathetic friend.   His own tastes were those of the scholar, and more and more, during the long Canadian winters, he enjoyed evenings of quiet reading.   The elder Mirabeau, father of the revolutionary leader of 1789, had just published his *Ami des Hommes* and this we find Montcalm studying.   But above all he reads the great encyclopædia of Diderot.   By 1759 seven of the huge volumes had been issued.   They startled the intellectual world of the time and Montcalm set out to read them, omitting the articles which had no interest for him or which he could not understand.   C is a copious letter in an encyclopædia, and Montcalm found excellent the articles on Christianity, College, Comedy, Comet, Commerce, Council, and so on.   Wolfe — soon to be his opponent — had the same taste for letters.   The two men, unlike in body, for Wolfe was tall and Montcalm the opposite, were alike in spirit, painstaking students as well as men of action.

At first Montcalm had not realized what was the deepest shadow in the life of Canada. Perhaps chiefly because Vaudreuil was always at Montreal, Montcalm preferred Quebec and was surprised and charmed by the life of that city. It had, he said, the air of a real capital. There were fair women and brave men, sumptuous dinners with forty or fifty covers, brilliantly lighted *salons*, a vivid social life in which he was much courted. The Intendant Bigot was agreeable and efficient. Soon, however, Montcalm had misgivings. It was a gambling age, but he was staggered by the extent of the gambling at the house of the Intendant. He did not wish to break with Bigot, and there was perhaps some weakness in his failure to denounce the orgies from which his conscience revolted. He warned his own officers but he could not control the colonial officers, and Vaudreuil was too weak to check a man like Bigot. Whence came the money? In time, Montcalm understood well enough. He himself was poor. To discharge the duties of his position he was going into debt, and he had even to consider the possible selling of his establishment in France. He had to beg the court for some financial relief. At the same time he saw about him a wild extravagance. There was famine in Canada. During the winter of 1758–59 the troops were put on short rations and, in spite of their bitter protests, had to eat horse flesh. Suffering and starvation bore heavily on the poor. Through lack of food people fell fainting in the streets. But the circle of Bigot paid little heed and feasted, danced, and gambled. Montcalm pours out his soul to Bourlamaque. He spends, he says, sleepless nights, and his mind is almost disordered by what he sees. In his journal he notes his own fight with poverty and its contrast with the careless luxury of a crowd of worthless hangers-on making four or five hundred thousand francs a year and insulting decency by their lavish expenditure. One of the ring, a clerk with a petty salary, a base creature, spends more on carriages, horses, and harness than a foppish and reckless young member of the *nouveaux-riches* would spend in France. Corruption in Canada is protected by corruption in France. Montcalm cries out with a devotion which his sovereign hardly deserved, though it was due to France herself, "O King, worthy of better service, dear France, crushed by taxes to enrich greedy knaves!"

The weary winter of 1758–59 at length came to an end. In May the ships already mentioned arrived from France, bringing Bougainville and, among other things, the news that Pitt was sending great forces for a decisive attack on Canada. At that very moment, indeed, the British ships were entering the mouth of the St. Lawrence. Canada had already been cut off from France. Montcalm held many councils with his officers. The strategy decided upon was to stand at bay at Quebec, to strike the enemy if he should try to land, and to hold out until the approach of winter should force the retirement of the British fleet.

14

CHAPTER X

THE STRATEGY OF PITT

DURING four campaigns the British had suffered humiliating disasters. It is the old story in English history of caste privilege and deadly routine bringing to the top men inadequate in the day of trial. It has happened since, even in our own day, as it has happened so often before. It seems that imminent disaster alone will arouse the nation to its best military effort. In 1757, however, England was thoroughly aroused. Failure then on her own special element, the sea, touched her vitally. Admiral Byng — through sheer cowardice, as was charged — had failed to attack a French fleet aiding in the siege of the island of Minorca which was held by the English, and Minorca had fallen to the French. Such was the popular clamor at this disaster that Byng was tried, condemned, and shot. There was also an upheaval in the government. At no time in English history were men more eager for the fruits of office; and now, even in a great crisis, the greed for spoils could not be shaken off. The nation demanded a conduct of the war which sought efficiency above all else. The politicians, however, insisted on government favors.

In the end a compromise was reached. At the head of the government was placed a politician, the Duke of Newcastle, who loved jobbery and patronage in politics and who doled out offices to his supporters. At the War Office was placed Pitt with a free hand to carry on military operations. He was the terrible cornet of horse who had harried Walpole in the days when that minister was trying to keep out of war. He knew and even loved war; his fierce national pride had been stirred to passion by the many humiliations at the hand of France; and now he was resolved to organize, to spend, and to fight, until Britain trampled on France. He had the nation behind him. He bullied and frightened the House of Commons. Members trembled if Pitt turned on them. By his fiery energy, by making himself a terror to weakness and incompetence, he won for Britain the Seven Years' War.

Though Pitt became Secretary of State for War in June, 1757, not until 1758 did the tide begin to turn in America. But when it did turn, it flowed with resistless force. In little more than a year the doom of New France was certain. The first great French reverse was at a point where the naval and military power of Britain could unite in attack. Pitt well understood the need of united action by the two services. Halifax became the radiating center of British activities. Here, in 1757, before Pitt was well in the saddle, a fleet and an army gathered to attack Louisbourg — an enterprise not carried out that year partly because France had a great fleet on the spot, and partly, too, on account of the bad quality of British leadership.

Only in the campaign of 1758 did Pitt's dominance become effective. With him counted one quality and one alone, efficiency. The old guard at the War Office were startled when men with rank, years, influence, and every other claim but competence for their tasks, were passed over, and young and obscure men were given high command. To America in the spring of 1758 were sent officers hitherto little known. Edward Boscawen, Commander of the Fleet, and veteran among these leaders, was a comparatively young man, only forty-seven; Jeffrey Amherst, just

turned forty, was Commander-in-Chief on land.
Next in command to Amherst was James Wolfe,
aged thirty.

These young and vigorous men knew the value
of promptness or they would not have been toler-
ated under Pitt. Before the end of May, 1758,
Boscawen was in Halifax harbor with a fleet of
some forty warships and a multitude of transports.
On board were nearly twelve thousand soldiers,
more than eleven thousand of them British regulars. The colonial forces now play a minor part
in the struggle; Pitt was ready to send from England all the troops needed. The array at Halifax,
the greatest yet seen in America, numbered about
twenty thousand men, including sailors. Before
the first of June the fleet was on its way to Louisbourg. The defense was stubborn; and James
Wolfe, who led the first landing party, had abundant opportunity to prove his courage and capacity. By the end of July, however, Louisbourg
had fallen, and nearly six thousand prisoners were
in the hands of the English. It was the beginning
of the end.

In the autumn Wolfe was back in England,
where he was quickly given command of the great
expedition which was planned against Quebec for

the following year. Admiral Sir Charles Saunders, who seems almost old compared with Wolfe, for he was nearly fifty, was in chief command of the fleet. Amherst had remained in America as Commander-in-Chief, and was taking slow, deliberate, thorough measures for the last steps in the conquest of New France.

To be too late had been the usual fate of the many British expeditions against Canada. No one, however, dared to be late under Pitt. On February 17, 1759, the greatest fleet that had ever put out for America left Portsmouth. More than two hundred and fifty ships set their sails for the long voyage. There were forty-nine warships, carrying fourteen thousand sailors and marines, and two hundred other ships manned by perhaps seven thousand men in the merchant service, but ready to fight if occasion offered. Altogether nearly thirty thousand men now left the shores of England to attack Canada.

There is a touch of doom for France in the fact that its own lost fortress of Louisbourg was to be the rendezvous of the fleet. Saunders, however, arrived so early that the entrance to Louisbourg was still blocked with ice, and he went on to Halifax. In time he returned to Louisbourg,

and from there the great fleet sailed for Quebec.
The voyage was uneventful. We can picture the
startled gaze of the Canadian peasants as they
saw the stately array, many miles long, pass up
the St. Lawrence. On the 26th of June, Wolfe
and Saunders were in the basin before Quebec and
the great siege had begun which was to mark one
of the turning-points in history.

Nature had furnished a noble setting for the
drama now to be enacted. Quebec stands on a
bold semicircular rock on the north shore of the
St. Lawrence. At the foot of the rock sweeps the
mighty river, here at the least breadth in its whole
course, but still a flood nearly a mile wide, deep and
strong. Its currents change ceaselessly with the
ebb and flow of the tide which rises a dozen feet,
though the open sea is eight hundred miles away.
Behind the rock of Quebec the small stream of the
St. Charles furnishes a protection on the landward
side. Below the fortress, the great river expands
into a broad basin with the outflow divided by the
Island of Orleans. In every direction there are
cliffs and precipices and rising ground. From the
north shore of the great basin the land slopes
gradually into a remote blue of wooded mountains. The assailant of Quebec must land on low

ground commanded everywhere from heights for seven or eight miles on the east and as many on the west. At both ends of this long front are further natural defenses — at the east the gorge of the Montmorency River, at the west that of the Cap Rouge River.

Wolfe's desire was to land his army on the Beauport shore at some point between Quebec and Montmorency. But Montcalm's fortified posts, behind which lay his army, stretched along the shore for six miles, all the way from the Montmorency to the St. Charles. Wolfe had a great contempt for Montcalm's army — "five feeble French battalions mixed with undisciplined peasants." If only he could get to close quarters with the "wily and cautious old fox," as he called Montcalm! Already the British had done what the French had thought impossible. Without pilots they had steered their ships through treacherous channels in the river and through the dangerous "Traverse" near Cap Tourmente. Captain Cook, destined to be a famous navigator, was there to survey and mark the difficult places, and British skippers laughed at the forecasts of disaster made by the pilots whom they had captured on the river. The French were confident that the British would not dare to take their ships farther up the river past the cannonade of the guns in Quebec, though this the British accomplished almost without loss.

Wolfe landed a force upon the lower side of the gorge at Montmorency and another at the head of the Island of Orleans. He planted batteries at Point Levis across the river from Quebec, and from there he battered the city. The pleasant houses in the Rue du Parloir which Montcalm knew so well were knocked into rubbish, and its fascinating ladies were driven desolate from the capital. But this bombardment brought Wolfe no nearer his goal. On the 31st of July he made a frontal attack on the flats at Beauport and failed disastrously with a loss of four hundred men. Time was fighting for Montcalm.

By the 1st of September Wolfe's one hope was in a surprise by which he could land an army above Quebec, the nearer to the fortress the better. Its feeble walls on the landward side could not hold out against artillery. But Bougainville guarded the high shore and marched his men incessantly up and down to meet threatened attacks. On the heights, the battalion of Guienne was encamped on the Plains of Abraham to guard the Foulon. This was a cove on the river bank from which there was a path, much used by the French for dragging up provisions, leading to the top of the cliff at a point little more than a mile from the walls of the city. On the 6th of September the battalion of Guienne was sent back to the Beauport lines by order of Vaudreuil. Montcalm countermanded the order, but was not obeyed, and Wolfe saw his chance. For days he threatened a landing, above and below Quebec, now at one point, now at another, until the French were both mystified and worn out with incessant alarms. Then, early on the morning of the 13th of September, came Wolfe's master-stroke. His men embarked in boats from the war-ships lying some miles above Quebec, dropped silently down the river, close to the north shore, made sentries believe that they were French boats carrying provisions to the Foulon, landed at the appointed spot, climbed up the cliff, and overpowered the sleeping guard. A little after daylight Wolfe had nearly five thousand soldiers, a "thin red line," busy preparing a strong position on the Plains of Abraham, while the fleet was landing cannon to be dragged up the steep hill to bombard the fortress on its weakest side.

Montcalm had spent many anxious days. He

had been incessantly on the move, examining for
himself over and over again every point, Cap
Rouge, Beauport, Montmorency, reviewing the
militia of which he felt uncertain, inspecting the
artillery, the commissariat, everything that mattered. At three o'clock in the morning of one of
these days he wrote to Bourlamaque, at Lake
Champlain, noting the dark night, the rain, his
men awake and dressed in their tents, everyone
alert. "I am booted and my horses are saddled,
which is in truth my usual way of spending the
night. I have not undressed since the twenty-
third of June." On the evening of the 12th of
September the batteries at Point Levis kept up a
furious fire on Quebec. There was much activity
on board the British war-ships lying below the
town. Boats filled with men rowed towards Beauport as if to attempt a landing during the night.
Here the danger seemed to lie. At midnight the
British boats were still hovering off the shore.
The French troops manned the entrenched lines
and Montcalm was continually anxious. A heavy
convoy of provisions was to come down to the
Foulon that night, and orders had been given to
the French posts on the north shore above Quebec
to make no noise. The arrival of the convoy was

vital, for the army was pressed for food. Montcalm was therefore anxious for its fate when at break of day he heard firing from the French cannon at Samos, above Quebec. Had the provisions then been taken by the English? Near his camp all now seemed quiet. He gave orders for the troops to rest, drank some cups of tea with his aide-de-camp Johnstone, a Scotch Jacobite, and at about half-past six rode towards Quebec to the camp of Vaudreuil to learn why the artillery was firing at Samos. Immediately in front of the Governor's house he learned the momentous news. The English were on the Plains of Abraham. Soon he had the evidence of his own eyes. On the distant heights across the valley he could see the redcoats.

No doubt Montcalm had often pondered this possibility and had decided in such a case to attack at once before the enemy could entrench and bring up cannon. A rapid decision was now followed by rapid action. He had a moment's conversation with Vaudreuil. The French regiments on the right at Vaudreuil's camp, lying nearest to the city, were to march at once. To Johnstone he said, "The affair is serious," and then gave orders that all the French left, except a few men to guard the ravine at Montmorency, should follow quickly to the position between Quebec and the enemy, a mile away. Off to this point he himself galloped. Already, by orders of officers on the spot, regiments were gathering between the walls of the city and the British. The regiments on the French right at Beauport were soon on the move towards the battlefield, but two thousand of the best troops still lay inactive beyond Beauport. Johnstone declares that Vaudreuil countermanded the order of Montcalm for these troops to come to his support and ordered that not one of them should budge. There was haste everywhere. By half-past nine Montcalm had some four thousand men drawn up between the British and the walls of Quebec. He hoped that Bougainville, advancing from Cap Rouge, would be able to assail the British rear: "Surely Bougainville understands that I must attack."

The crisis was over in fifteen minutes. Montcalm attacked at once. His line was disorderly. His center was composed of regular troops, his wings of Canadians and Indians. These fired irregularly and lay down to reload, thus causing confusion. The French moved forward rapidly; the British were coming on more slowly. The French were only some forty yards away when

there was an answering fire from the thin red line;
for Wolfe had ordered his men to put two balls in
their muskets and to hold their fire for one dread
volley. Then the roar from Wolfe's center was
like that of a burst of artillery; and, when the
smoke cleared, the French battalions were seen
breaking in disorder from the shock, the front line
cut down by the terrible fire. A bayonet charge
from the redcoats followed. Some five thousand
trained British regulars bore down, working great
slaughter on four thousand French, many of them
colonials who had never before fought in the open.
The rout of the French was complete. Some fled
to safety behind the walls of Quebec, others down
the Côte Ste. Geneviève and across the St. Charles
River, where they stopped pursuit by cutting the
bridge. Both Wolfe and Montcalm were mortally
wounded after the issue of the day was really
decided, and both survived to be certain, the one
of victory, the other of defeat. Wolfe died on the
field of battle. Montcalm was taken into a house
in Quebec and died early the next morning. It is
perhaps the only incident in history of a decisive
battle of world import followed by the death of
both leaders, each made immortal by the tragedy
of their common fate.

At two o'clock in the afternoon of the day of defeat, Vaudreuil held a tumultuous council of war. It was decided to abandon Quebec, where Montcalm lay dying and to retreat up the St. Lawrence to Montreal, to the defense of which Lévis had been sent before the fight. That night the whole French army fled in panic, leaving their tents standing and abandoning quantities of stores. Vaudreuil who had talked so bravely about death in the ruins of Canada, rather than surrender, gave orders to Ramezay, commanding in Quebec, to make terms and haul down his flag. On the third day after the battle, the surrender was arranged. On the fourth day the British marched into Quebec, where ever since their flag has floated.

Meanwhile, Amherst, the Commander-in-Chief of the British armies in America, was making a toilsome advance towards Montreal by way of Lake Champlain. He had occupied both Ticonderoga and Crown Point, which had been abandoned by the French. Across his path lay Bourlamaque at Isle aux Noix. Another British army, having captured Niagara, was advancing on Montreal down the St. Lawrence from Lake Ontario. Amherst, however, made little progress this year in his menace to Montreal and soon went into winter quarters, as did the other forces elsewhere. The British victory therefore was as yet incomplete.

The year 1759 proved dire for France. She was held fast by her treaty with Austria and at ruinous cost was ever sending more and more troops to help Austria against Prussia. The great plan of which Belle-Isle had written to Montcalm was the chief hope of her policy. England was to be invaded and London occupied. If this were done, all else would be right. It was not done. France could not parry Pitt's blows. In Africa, in the West Indies, in India, the British won successes which meant the ruin of French power in three continents. French admirals like Conflans and La Clue were no match for Boscawen, Hawke, and Rodney, all seamen of the first rank, and made the stronger because dominated by the fiery Pitt. They kept the French squadrons shut up in their own ports. When, at last, on November 20, 1759, Conflans came out of Brest and fought Hawke at Quiberon Bay, the French fleet was nearly destroyed, and the dream of taking London ended in complete disaster.

CHAPTER XI

THE FALL OF CANADA

THOUGH Quebec was in their hands, the position of the British during the winter of 1759–60 was dangerous. In October General Murray, who was left in command, saw with misgiving the great fleet sail away which had brought to Canada the conquering force of Wolfe and Saunders. Murray was left with some seven thousand men in the heart of a hostile country, and with a resourceful enemy, still unconquered, preparing to attack him. He was separated from other British forces by vast wastes of forest and river, and until spring should come no fleet could aid him. Three enemies of the English, the French said exultingly, would aid to retake Quebec: the ruthless savages who haunted the outskirts of the fortress and massacred many an incautious straggler; the French army which could be recruited from the Canadian population; and, above all, the bitter cold of the Canadian winter. To Murray, as to Napoleon long afterward in his rash invasion of Russia, General February was indeed the enemy. About the two or three British ships left at Quebec the ice froze in places a dozen feet thick, and snowdrifts were piled so high against the walls of Quebec that it looked sometimes as if the enemy might walk over them into the fortress. So solidly frozen was the surface of the river that Murray sent cannon to the south shore across the ice to repel a menace from that quarter. There was scarcity of firewood and of provisions. Scurvy broke out in the garrison. Many hundreds died so that by the spring Murray had barely three thousand men fit for active duty.

Throughout the winter Lévis, now in command of the French forces, made increasing preparations to destroy Murray in the spring. The headquarters of Lévis were at Montreal. Here Vaudreuil, the Governor, kept his little court. He and Lévis worked harmoniously, for Lévis was conciliatory and tactful. For a time Vaudreuil treasured the thought of taking command in person to attack Quebec. In the end, however, he showed that he had learned something from the disasters of the previous year and did not interfere with the

plans made by Lévis. So throughout the winter
Montreal had its gayeties and vanities as of old.
There were feasts and dances — but over all
brooded the reality of famine in the present and
the foreboding of disaster to come.

By April 20, 1760, the St. Lawrence was open
and, though the shores were cumbered with masses
of broken ice, the central channel was free for the
boats which Lévis filled with his soldiers. It was a
bleak experience to descend the turbulent river
between banks clogged with ice. When Lévis
was not far from Quebec, he learned that it was
impossible to surprise Murray who was well on
guard between Cap Rouge on the west and Beauport on the east. The one thing to do was to reach
the Plains of Abraham in order to attack the
feeble walls of Quebec from the landward side.
Since Murray's alertness made impossible attack
by way of the high cliffs which Wolfe had climbed
in the night, Lévis had to reach Quebec by a cir-
cuitous route. He landed his army a little above
Cap Rouge, marched inland over terrible roads in
heavy rain, and climbed to the plateau of Quebec
from the rear at Sainte Foy. On April 27, 1760,
he drew up his army on the heights almost exactly
as Wolfe had done in the previous September.

Murray followed the example of Montcalm. He had no trust in the feeble defenses of Quebec and on the 28th marched out to fight on the open plain. The battle of Sainte Foy followed exactly the precedents of the previous year. The defenders of Quebec were driven off the field in overwhelming defeat. The difference was that Murray took his army back to Quebec and from behind its walls still defied his French assailant. Lévis had poor artillery, but he did what he could. He entrenched and poured his fire into Quebec. In the end it was sea power which balked him. On the 15th of May, when a British fleet appeared round the head of the Island of Orleans, Lévis withdrew in something like panic and Quebec was safe.

Lévis returned to Montreal; and to this point all the forces of France slowly retreated as they were pressed in by the overwhelming numbers of the British. At Oswego, the scene of Montcalm's first brilliant success four years earlier, Amherst had gathered during the summer of 1760 an army of about ten thousand men. From here he descended the St. Lawrence in boats to attack Montreal from the west. From the south, down Lake Champlain and the Richelieu River to the St. Lawrence, came another British force under Haviland also to attack Montreal. At Quebec Murray put his army on transports, left the city almost destitute of defense, and thus brought a third considerable force against Montreal. There was little fighting. The French withdrew to the common objective as their enemy advanced. Early in September Lévis had gathered at Montreal all his available force, amounting now to scarcely more than two thousand men, for Canadians and Indians alike had deserted him. The British pressed in with the slow and inevitable rigor of a force of nature. On the 7th of September their united army was before the town and Amherst demanded instant surrender. The only thing for Vaudreuil to do was to make the best terms possible. On the next day he signed a capitulation which protected the liberties in property and religion of the Canadians but which yielded the whole of Canada to Great Britain. The struggle for North America had ended.

In the moment of triumph Amherst inflicted on the French army a deep humiliation to punish the outrages committed by their Indian allies. In the early days of the war Loudoun, the Commander-in-Chief in America, had vowed that the British would make the French "sick of such inhuman villainy" and teach them to respect "the laws of nature and humanity." Washington speaks of his "deadly sorrow" at the dreadful outrages which he saw, the ravishing of women, the scalping alive even of children. Philadelphians had seen the grim spectacle of a wagon-load of corpses brought by mourning friends and relatives of the dead and laid down at the door of the Assembly to show to pacifist legislators what was really happening. The French regular officers, as we have seen, had hated this kind of warfare. Bougainville says that his soul shuddered at the sights in Montreal, where the whole town turned out to see an English prisoner killed, boiled, and eaten by the savages. Worse still, captive mothers were obliged to eat the flesh of their own children. The French believed that they could not get on without the savage allies who committed these outrages, and they were not strong enough to coerce them. Amherst, on the other hand, held his Indians in check and rebuked outrage. Now he was stern to punish what the French had permitted. He could write proudly to a friend that the French were amazed at the order in which he kept his own Indians. Not a man, woman, or child, he said, had been hurt or a single atrocity committed. It was a vivid contrast with what had taken place after the British surrender to Montcalm at Fort William Henry. The day of retribution had come. Because of such outrages, the French army was denied the honors of war usually conceded to a brave and defeated foe. The French officers and men must not, Amherst insisted, serve again during the war. Lévis protested and begged Vaudreuil to be allowed to go on fighting rather than accept the terms, but in vain. The humiliation was rigorously imposed, and it was a sullen host which the British took captive.

France had lost an Empire. It was nearly three years still before peace was signed at Paris in 1763. To Britain France yielded everything east of the Mississippi except New Orleans, and to Spain she ceded New Orleans and everything else to which she had any claim. The *fleurs-de-lis* floated still over only two tiny fishing islands off the Newfoundland shore. All the glowing plans of France's leaders — of Richelieu, of Louis XIV, of Colbert, of Frontenac, of the heroic missionaries of the Jesuit Order — seemed to have come to nothing.

The fall of France did much to drag down her rival. Already was America restless under control from Europe. There was now no danger to the English in America from the French peril which had made insecure the borders of Massachusetts, of New York, of Pennsylvania, and Virginia, and had brought widespread desolation and sorrow. With the removal of the menace went the need of help and defenses for the colonies from the motherland. The French belief that there was a natural antipathy between the English of the Old World and the English of the New was, in reality, based on the fact of a likeness so great that neither would accept control or patronage from the other. Towards the Englishman who assumed airs of superiority the antagonism of the colonists was always certain to be acute. Open strife came when the assumption of superiority took the form of levying taxes on the colonies without asking their leave. In no remote way the fall of French Canada, by removing a near menace to the English colonies, led to this new conflict and to the collapse of that older British Empire which had sprung from the England of the Stuarts.

When Montreal fell there were in the St. Lawrence many British ships which had been used for troops and supplies. Before the end of September the French soldiers and also the officials from

France who desired to go home were on board these ships bound for Europe. By the end of November most of the exiles had reached home. Varying receptions awaited them. Lévis, who took back the army, was soon again, by consent of the British government, in active service. Fortune smiled on him to the end. He died a great noble and Marshal of France just before the Revolution of 1789; but in that awful upheaval his widow and his two daughters perished on the scaffold. Vaudreuil's shallow and vain incompetence did not go unpunished. He was put on trial, accused of a share in the black frauds which had helped to ruin Canada. The trial was his punishment. He was acquitted of taking any share of the plunder and so drops out of history. Bigot and his gang, on the other hand, were found guilty of vast depredations. The former Intendant was for a time in the Bastille and in the end was banished from France, after being forced to repay great sums. We find echoes of the luxury of Quebec in the sale in France of the rich plate which the rascal had acquired. There were, however, other and even worse plunderers. They were tried and condemned chiefly to return what they had stolen. We rather wonder that no expiatory sacrifice on the scaffold was required of any of these knaves. Lally Tollendal, who, as the French leader in India, had only failed and not plundered, was sent to a cruel execution.

Under the terms of the surrender and of the final Treaty of Peace in 1763, civilians in Canada were given leave to return to France. Nearly the whole of the official class and many of the large land-owners, the seigneurs, left the country. In Canada there remained a priesthood, largely native, but soon to be recruited from France by the upheaval of the Revolution, a few seigneurial families, natural leaders of their race, a peasantry, exhausted by the long war but clinging tenaciously to the soil, and a good many hardy pioneers of the forest, men skilled in hunting and in the use of the axe. Out of these elements, amounting in 1763 to little more than sixty thousand people, has come that French-Canadian race in America now numbering perhaps three millions. The race has scattered far. It is found in the mills of Massachusetts, in the canebrakes of Louisiana, on the wide stretches of the prairie of the Canadian West, but it has always kept intact its strong citadel on the banks of the St. Lawrence. New France was, in reality, widely separated in spirit from old France, before the new master in Canada made the division permanent. The imagination of the Canadian peasant did not wander across the ocean to France. He knew only the scenes about his own hearth and in them alone were his thought and affections centered.

The one wider interest which the habitant treasured was love for the Catholic Church of his fathers and of his own spiritual hopes. It thus happened that when France in revolution assailed and for a time overthrew the Church within her borders, the heart of French Canada was not with France but with the persecuted Church; she hated the spirit of revolutionary France. *Te Deums* were sung at Quebec in thanksgiving for the defeats of Napoleon. In language and what literary culture they possessed, in traditions and tastes, the conquered people remained French, but they had no allegiance divided between Canada and France. To this day they are proud to be simply Canadians, rooted in the soil of Canada, with no debt of patriotic gratitude to the France from which they sprang or to the Britain which obtained political dominance over their ancestors after a long agony of war. To the British Crown many of them feel a certain attachment because of the liberty guaranteed to them to pursue their own ideals of happiness. In preserving their type of social life, their faith and language, they have shown a resolute tenacity. To this day they are as different in these things from their fellow-citizens of British origin in the rest of Canada as were their ancestors from the English colonies which lay on their borders.

The French in Canada are still a separate people. From time to time a nervous fear seizes them lest too many of their race may be lost to their old ideals in the Anglo-Saxon world surging about them. Then they listen readily to appeals to their racial unity and draw more sharply than ever the lines of division between themselves and the rest of North America. They remain a fragment of an older France, remote and isolated, still dreaming dreams like those of Frontenac of old of the dominance of their race in North America and asserting passionately their rights in the soil of Canada to which, first of Europeans, they came. At the mouth of the Mississippi in the Louisiana founded by Louis XIV, along the St. Lawrence in the Canada of Champlain and Frontenac, with a resolution more than half pathetic, and in a world that gives little heed, men of French race are still on guard to preserve in America the lineaments of that older France, long since decayed in Europe, which was above all the eldest daughter of the Church.

BIBLIOGRAPHICAL NOTE

While the present narrative is based for the most part on more recondite and widely scattered sources, the most accessible volumes relating to the period are the following works of Francis Parkman (Boston: many editions): *La Salle and the Discovery of the Great West, Frontenac and New France under Louis XIV, A Half Century of Conflict* (2 vols.), and *Montcalm and Wolfe* (2 vols.). To these should be added, as completing the story, George M. Wrong, *The Fall of Canada* (Oxford, 1914) which dwells in detail on the last year of the struggle. All these volumes contain adequate references to authorities. The last of Parkman's works was published more than twenty-five years ago and later research has revised some of his conclusions, but he still commands great authority. In *The Chronicles of Canada* (Toronto, 1913–16) half a dozen volumes relate to the period; each of these volumes, which embody later research and are written in an attractive style, contains a bibliography relating to its special subject: C. W. Colby, *The Fighting Governor* [Frontenac]; Agnes C. Laut, *The Adventurers of England on Hudson Bay;* Lawrence J. Burpee, *The Pathfinders of the Great Plains;* Arthur G. Doughty, *The Acadian Exiles;* William Wood, *The Great Fortress* [Louisbourg], *The*

Passing of New France, and *The Winning of Canada*. Lawrence J. Burpee's *Search for the Western Sea* (Toronto, 1908) deals with the work of La Vérendrye and other explorers. Anthony Hendry's *Journal* is published in the *Transactions of the Royal Society of Canada*, series iii, volume i. The latest phase of the discussions on La Vérendrye are reviewed in an article by Doane Robinson in *The Mississippi Valley Historical Review* for December, 1916. The material relating to the discoverer was long scattered, but it has now been collected in a volume, edited by Lawrence J. Burpee for the Champlain Society, Toronto, but owing to the war it is at the present date (1918) still in manuscript. Much of what is contained in Mr. Burpee's volume will be found in *South Dakota Historical Collections*, volume vii, 1914 (Pierre, S. D.).

Additional references are given in the bibliographies appended to the articles on *Chatham, Seven Years' War*, and *Nova Scotia* in *The Encyclopædia Britannica*, 11th Edition.

INDEX

Abenaki Indians, incited against English, 76

Abercromby, James, General, 195–96

Acadia, settled by French, 2; comes into hands of British, 56; ceded to England, 65; conditions in (1713), 74–75; England's neglect of, 75; expulsion of Acadians, 164 *et seq.*; boundaries undefined, 169

Aix-la-Chapelle, Peace of (1748), 93

Albany, plan to seize, 12; colonial delegates meet at (1754), 159–60

Alsace-Lorraine, demanded of France, 64

Amherst, Jeffrey, Commander-in-Chief of British forces in America, 195, 213, 214; advances toward Montreal, 223; attacks Montreal, 228–29; relations with Indians, 230

Andros, Sir Edmund, 34

Annapolis, attacked by French, 79–80; Acadians driven from, 175

Annapolis Valley, 53

Anne, Queen, ascends throne, 45; intrigue in court, 56–57; death (1714), 67

Anson, George, Admiral, 92

Anville, Duc d', 90, 91

Argall, Samuel, Captain, 2

Assiniboine Indians, accompany La Vérendrye, 121, 122–23

Assiniboine River, 119–20

Auguste, The (ship), 133

Austrian Succession, War of (1744–48), 71, 92–93, 155

Beauharnois, Marquis de, Governor of Canada, 114

Beauséjour, Fort, 170, 171, 172

Belle-Isle, Duc de, French Minister of War, 201

Berryer, French Minister of Marine, 200–01

Bienville, J. B. le Moyne, Sieur de, 104

Big Mouth, Indian, 6

Bigot, François, Intendant of Canada, 185, 203, 207, 233

Biloxi Bay, fort built on, 103

Blackfeet Indians, 140–41

Bobé, Father, 26

Boscawen, Edward, Admiral, 158, 163, 212, 213

Boston, plan to seize, 46

Bougainville, L. A. de, Colonel, 181–82, 199–200, 217, 230

Bouquet, Henry, Colonel, 163

Bourlamaque, Chevalier de, 181, 191, 223

Bow Indians, act as guides to the La Vérendryes, 126–28

Braddock, Edward, General, 158, 159, 160

Byng, Admiral, 146, 210

Cadet, Head of Canadian supplies department, 203

Canada, paternal government in, 24–25; war on English colonies, 45 *et seq*.; English plans for ending French power in, 87–88; corruption in, 203–204, 207–08; famine in, 208; population (1763), 234; French Canadians, 235–37

Canada and English colonies compared, as to population, 35; finances, 35–37; leaders, 37–38; governors, 39; religion, 40–41; education, 42; books and newspapers, 42–43; character of people, 78

Canseau, taken by French, 79; British arrive at, 82

Cape Breton, Island of, 65, 72, 74

Cartier, Jacques, 98

Céloron de Blainville, 146 *et seq*.

Champlain, Samuel de, 100

Charles II, becomes King (1660), 28; of Catholic faith, 30; intrigues with France, 31; Catholic persecution under, 31; death (1685), 33

Charlevoix, P. F. X. de, 45, 104, 112

Chautauqua Lake, 149

Clarendon, Earl of, Governor of N. J. and N. Y., 39

Cook, James, Captain, 216

Cornwallis, Edward, 95

Crown Point, French army at, 161; occupied by British, 223

Deerfield Massacre, 46–48

Denonville, Marquis de, Governor of Canada, 9

Detroit, fort built at, 105–06

Dieskau, Baron, 158, 161, 162, 179–80

Digby Basin, 53

Dinwiddie, Robert, Lieutenant-Governor of Va., 153, 154, 160

Duchesneau, Jacques, Intendant of Canada, 28

Duchambon, Governor of Louisbourg, 82, 84

Duquesne, Governor of Canada, 152

Duquesne, Fort, 154, 160, 163, 198

Duvivier, 79

Edgar, The (ship), 59, 61

Edward, Fort, 193, 194

England, Protestant, 1; attitude toward her colonies, 25; under Charles II, 28; protection from France, 29–30; reduces army, 44; war with France, 45; success on the sea, 92; sends army to Va., 158; relations with colonies 232

Estournel, d', 91

Europe, politics in middle eighteenth century, 155–57

Forbes, John, General, 163

France, Catholic, 1; treatment of colonies by, 24–25; claims in North America, 26–27; persecution of Protestants, 32–33; failure in war in Europe, 64; cedes part of Canada to England, 65; fails in plans against English, 90–92; lays claim to the West, 98 *et seq*.; allies herself to Austria, 156–57; sends army to Canada, 158; plans invasion of England, 201; fails in undertakings of 1759, 224; yields everything east of Mississippi, 231

Franklin, Benjamin, 160

Frontenac, Louis de Buade, Comte de, Governor of Canada, family, 3; personal characteristics, 3–5; in Canada, 4–5; commands against Iroquois, 9–12; against English, 12–15; deals with Phips' expedition, 18–20; leads against Iroquois, 22; death (1698), 22

Frontenac, Fort, 148, 198
Fur trade, government monopoly, 40; on Hudson Bay, 108, 135–36

George I, becomes King (1714), 67; policy toward France, 67
George II, demands oath of allegiance from Acadians, 165
George, Fort, 161
Gibraltar, ceded to England, 68
Grand Pré, 175–76

Halifax, founded, 94–96, 147; importance to British, 167; center of activities, 212
Harvard College, organized (1638), 42
Hayes, Fort, 109
Hendry, Anthony, 136 et seq., 161, 240
Henry, Alexander, 139–40
Hill, "Jack," General, 57, 61
Howe, Captain, 171
Howe, Lord, 196
Hudson Bay, ceded to England, 65; English traders on, 108–110; French attacks, 109–10
Hudson's Bay Company, 108, 135
Huron Indians, allies of French, 11; Jesuit mission to, 100

Iberville, Pierre Le Moyne, Sieur d', 37–38, 103, 109–10
Indians, pit English against French, 6–7; trade with, 7–8; Frontenac seeks alliance with, 14; French meet at Ste. Marie du Saut, 101–02; French gain support of, 161; Montcalm's relations with, 183–84; allies of French, 187–88, 192; Amherst's discipline of, 230–31; see also names of tribes.
Iroquois Indians, five tribes, 8; hostile to French, 8–15; village destroyed by Frontenac,

22; become British subjects, 45; raid on Lachine, 48; menace Niagara, 105; British claim lands of, 151; nervous for their safety, 159–60
Isle aux Noix, 223

James II, 33–34
Jenkins, Captain, 71
Johnson, Sir William, 159, 161–162
Johnstone, aide-de-camp to Montcalm, 220, 221
Joliet, Louis, 102
Jumonville, Coulon de, 154, 155

King George's War (1743–48), Canseau captured, 79; Annapolis attacked, 79–80; expedition against Louisbourg, 80–87; plan to end French power in America, 88; Louisbourg under the English, 88–90; France fails to retake Louisbourg, 90–93; treaty of peace (1748), 93; see also Austrian Succession, War of

Lachine, Massacre at, 9, 48
La Corne, St. Luc de, 135, 136, 141
La Galissonière, Marquis de, acting Governor of Canada, 146
La Jemeraye, 118
La Jonquière, Marquis de, Governor of Canada, 91, 92
La Jonquière, Fort, 134, 135, 138
La Mothe Cadillac, Antoine de, 105–06
La Pause, officer under Montcalm, 191
La Porte, 204
La Potherie, describes council with Indians, 11–12
La Reine, Fort, 120, 121, 124, 125, 133, 134

La Salle, Rene-Robert Cavelier, Sieur de, 103
Laval University, 42
La Vérendrye, P. G. de Varennes, Sieur de, 110 *et seq.*, 240
La Vérendrye brothers, 125–33
Lawrence, Charles, Major, 173
Lawrence, Fort, 170, 171, 172
Le Bœuf, Fort, 152, 153
Le Loutre, Abbe, 167 *et seq.*
Le Mercier, officer under Montcalm, 191
Le Moyne, Charles, 37
Lévis, Chevalier de, next Montcalm in command, 181; suggested as Montcalm's successor by Governor, 186; at Montreal, 223, 226; attempts to retake Quebec, 227–28; defeat at Montreal, 228–29; becomes Marshal of France, 233
Lewis and Clark expedition, 143
Loudoun, Earl of, Commander-in-Chief of British, 193, 229
Louis XIV, attitude toward Canada, 24–25
Louisbourg, fortress built, 72–74; plan for capture of, 80–81; conditions in, 81–82; siege of, 82–85; English in, 88–90; treaty of Aix-la-Chapelle restores to France, 93; expedition against, 193; fall of fortress, 195; capture of, 213; rendezvous of British fleet, 214
Louisiana Purchase, 143

Mackenzie, Alexander, 142–43
Mackenzie River, 97, 142
Malartic, officer under Montcalm, 191
Mandan Indians, 122, 123–24, 125–26
Marquette, Jacques, Jesuit priest, 102–03
Mars, The (ship), 90
Mascarene, Paul, 80
Massachusetts, sends expedi-

tions against French, 17–21; religion, 40; offers bounty for Indian scalps, 48; war with Indians (1721), 77
Maurepas, Fort, at Biloxi, 103; on Lake Winnipeg, 107, 118, 133
Mayflower, The (ship), 25
Michilimackinac, 100
Micmac Indians, 167, 171
Mississippi River, 97–98, 99, 102–03
Monckton, Robert, Colonel, 174
Monro, George, Colonel, 193
Montcalm, Louis Joseph, Marquis de, life in France, 178–79; sent to Canada, 179; voyage, 180–81; staff, 181–82; impressions of Canada, 182–83; attitude toward Indians, 183–84; Vaudreuil jealous of, 185–86; activities in Canada, 189–90; captures Oswego, 190; describes his officers, 191; at Ticonderoga, 192; captures Fort William Henry, 192–93; rebuked by French court, 194; defeats British at Lake George, 195–97; plans organization of army, 198–99; fame in France, 200; obtains little aid from France, 202; receives rank of Lieutenant-General, 202; a hero, 204–05; personal characteristics, 205–06; discovers corruption of Canadian officials, 207–08; plans to meet British attack, 209; at siege of Quebec, 218–22
Montigny, officer under Montcalm, 191
Montreal, war party sets out from, 14; Lévis at, 223, 226; French defeat at, 228–29
Murray, James, General, 225–228, 229

Nantes, Edict of, 32
Nepigon, 113

New France, *see* Canada

New Netherland captured by English (1664), 12

New Orleans, 104, 148, 231

New York, plan of French to capture, 12–14; sends force against French (1691), 21–22

Newcastle, Duke of, 211

Newfoundland, ceded to England, 65

Niagara, Fort, 105, 148, 223

Nicholson, Francis, Colonel, 51, 52, 53, 63

Niverville, Chevalier de, 133–34

Nova Scotia, *see* Acadia

Noyon, 112

Oates, Titus, 31

Ochagach, Indian guide, 113, 114

Ohio River, importance to French, 106, 147–48; Céloron on, 149–50; contest for possession, 150–63

Oswego, French plans to capture, 189; captured, 190; Amherst gathers army at, 228

Paddon, Captain, of the *Edgar*, 59

Panama, Isthmus of, Scottish attempt to found colony on, 49

Paskoya, Fort, 134, 136

Pelican, The (ship), 110

Pennsylvania, policy of non-resistance, 35–36; Quakers in, 40; suffers from French and Indians, 152

Pepperrell, William, 82–83, 89

Phips, Sir William, Governor of Mass., 15–16; raises Spanish wreck, 16; leads expedition against Acadia, 17; voyages to Quebec, 18–21; not fitted to office, 38; superstitions of, 41

Pierre, S. D., tablet of the La Vérendryes found at, 128–29

Pisiquid (Windsor), 175

Pitt, William, British Secretary of State for War, 195, 211 *et seq.*

"Pitts-Bourgh," 163

Pompadour, Madame de, 156, 178, 199–200

Port Royal, captured by Phips, 17; typical French community, 54; captured by English, 55–56; renamed Annapolis, 55

Porto Bello, 70

Prince Edward Island, 65

Quebec, captured by English, 2; war party sets out from, 14; Phips takes fleet to, 18–21; child of Versailles, 24; expedition against (1711), 57–63; life in, 207; situation of, 215–16; siege of, 217–22; French defeat at, 222, 227–28

Rainy Lake, 115, 118

Rale, Sebastien, Jesuit priest, 76, 77

Ramezay, Chevalier de, 223

Red River, 119

Rigaud, brother of Governor Vaudreuil, 191

Rouville, Hertel de, 46–47

Ryswick, Peace of (1697), 22–23, 44

St. Charles, Fort, 115, 116, 118

St. Esprit, 101

St. Jean, Ile, 65

St. Lawrence River, French pioneers on, 97–98; location, 99; cities on, 100; British fleet sails up, 215

St. Louis, Château, 5, 19, 38

Saint Luc, officer under Montcalm, 191

Saint-Lusson, S. F. Daumont, Sieur de, 101

Saint-Pierre, Legardeur de, 131–132, 133–35, 150–51, 153, 162

St. Pierre, Fort, 115
Saint-Sauveur, Grasset de, 203
Sainte Foy, Battle of, 228
Ste. Marie du Saut, 100, 101
Saskatchewan River, 97–98
Saunders, Sir Charles, Admiral, 214
Schenectady, massacre at, 15
Schuyler, Peter, 21–22, 52
Seven Years' War, 151, 211
Shirley, William, Governor of Mass., 80, 81, 88, 173
Sioux Indians, 107, 119
South Sea Bubble, 70–71
Spain, cessions to England, 68, 69–70; relations with England, 71; England hostile to, 92, 93; claims lands on Gulf of Mexico, 99; New Orleans ceded to, 231
Subercase, D. A. de, Governor of Port Royal, 54, 55

Three Rivers, war party sets out from, 14
Ticonderoga, French army at, 161; Montcalm at, 192, 195, 196; defeat of English at, 196–197; occupied by British, 223
Tollendal, Lally, 234
Troyes, Chevalier de, 109

Utrecht, Treaty of (1713), 64–66, 110

Vaudreuil, Pierre de Rigaud, Marquis de, Governor of Canada, values Indians as allies, 183; as Governor, 184–85; jealous of Montcalm, 185–86, 203; in hands of corrupt circle, 203–04; retreats to

Montreal, 223, 226; signs capitulation, 229; trial of, 233
Vaughan, William, 80
Verrazano, sails along Atlantic coast (1524), 26
Vetch, Samuel, plans conquest of Canada, 49–52, adjutant-general, 53; made Governor of Annapolis, 55; commands colonial forces, 58; familiar with St. Lawrence, 61; in debtor's prison, 62
Vigilant, The (ship), 85
Virginia, settled (1607), 2; Church of England in, 40

Walker, Sir Hovenden, Admiral, 57 *et seq.*
Walpole, Sir Robert, English Prime Minister. ʼ8–69
Warren, Peter, Commodore, 81, 83, 88, 89, 92
Washington, George, 151, 152 *et seq.*, 160, 163, 230
William of Orange, France denounces, 2, 20; recognized by France, 23; as King of England, 34, 44; death (1702), 45
William Henry, Fort, 161, 192–193
Williams, Rev. John, 47–48
Winnipeg, Lake, 117, 119
Winslow, Colonel, 175, 176
Witchcraft in New England, 41
Wolfe, James, General, at Louisbourg, 163, 195; compared with Montcalm, 206; next Amherst in command, 213; at Louisbourg, 213; at Quebec, 216–22
Woods, Lake of the, 112, 115